Shadows in the Night

Memoirs of a Ghost Hunter

Shadows in the Night

Memoirs of a Ghost Hunter

Diana Jarvis

BOOKS

Winchester, UK
Washington, USA

First published by O-Books, 2010
O-Books is an imprint of John Hunt Publishing Ltd., Laurel House, Station Approach,
Alresford, Hants, SO24 9JH, UK
office1@o-books.net
www.o-books.com

For distributor details and how to order please visit the 'Ordering' section on our website.

A CIP catalogue record for this book is available from the British Library.

Design: Tom Davies

Printed in the UK by CPI Antony Rowe
Printed in the USA by Offset Paperback Mfrs, Inc

We operate a distinctive and ethical publishing philosophy in all
areas of our business, from our global network of authors to
production and worldwide distribution.

CONTENTS

To Dorothy Boreman and 'Nemo'.
Wherever I am, you've helped me get there.
Sic transit...

To Gordon
Wherever I am, I'm glad I can share the experience with you.
...gloria mundi.

Acknowledgements

I would like to extend my thanks to a number of people for their help with this book.

Firstly, I'd like to thank accomplished author and paranormal investigator, Michael J Hallowell. Mike has been an inspiration to me with his professionalism, expertise, good humor and his genuine compassion for people. I am honored to have his name at the bottom of the Foreword and honored to call him a friend.

Secondly, my thanks go to my partner-in-crime, Rachel Lacy. She has been a friend and an invaluable support in both my professional and private life. She is also a dedicated and knowledgeable ghost investigator. What she doesn't know about the ghosts of York or about York's history isn't worth knowing. No ghost hunt is quite the same without her.

There are many investigators, witnesses and friends who need a mention, some of whom have been kind enough to add their own comments to the book. Their efforts and support have made ghost hunting possible for me, and without them, I would have nothing to write. In particular I'd like to offer thanks to *Amanda*, Simon Curwood, Carole Chui, Norie Miles, Dru Sinanan, James Littlewood, John Riley and Clare Dunn for their expertise. Sandie Riley is also deserving of a mention; especially as she accurately predicted that this book would reach the shelves – at least 10 years before it was conceived.

Every author needs opinions on their work. I have been lucky enough to have Paul Clay to thank for objective criticism, as well as help with the text. Further thanks in this regard must go to

O-Books. Without them, this book would not be on the shelves in the first place.

Thanks are also due to Gordon, my husband. He has encouraged me and believed in me from the day I first met him; and has been very supportive of my writing and my 'unusual' hobby. This book is dedicated in part to him. His support, coupled with that of the rest of my family, is invaluable. I am particularly grateful to my children: Robert, David, Fai and Jonathan. They have accepted their mother's / stepmother's eccentricity with good grace and humor, and their understanding is much appreciated. It's not easy explaining to your peers that your mother is a ghost-hunting witch!

Finally, I'd like to thank my spirit guides both past and present for their unseen help during all the events covered in this book: Mackay, for his drunken humor that keeps me laughing in the face of adversity; and Annaliese, whom I miss every single day.

Foreword

The philosopher Edmund Burke once said that, 'The only thing necessary for evil to triumph is for good men to do nothing.' Burke was right. My grandmother, on the other hand, once said that, 'The Devil finds work for idle hands', which pretty much amounts to the same thing in my book. From an early age, I a) wanted to do *something* with my life, and b) had no desire whatsoever to be a hand-servant of Beelzebub. The Devil doesn't care one jot for either equal opportunities or employment protection laws, and his pension scheme is just awful. Somehow, I resolved my moral and ethical dilemmas by writing books and investigating the supernatural. I'm not sure what the connection is, and wouldn't even attempt to justify it logically, but hunting down ghosts and aliens makes me feel better. There's probably a good case to be made here for me visiting a shrink, but I'm far too busy doing other things at the moment – like grappling with poltergeists and interviewing celebrity mediums.

As my career as a paranormal investigator blossomed, I was given the opportunity to write for a monthly glossy called *Vision*, which dealt with both the supernatural and what is generally referred to as 'alternative spirituality'. When Diana Jarvis took over the reins as editor, I was told that she was a veteran in the field and 'knew what she was doing'. This frightened the living daylights out of me, of course, because my chances of talking my way out of mistakes and errors of judgment – trust me, I've made a few – was thus reduced to zero. Seriously though, I needn't have worried. Diana turned out to be the finest editor I've ever

1

had the privilege of working with. She knew her subject matter intimately and made the magazine her own. As a columnist for *Vision* I developed a working relationship with Diana that persists to this day. We're also good friends, although *Vision* has unfortunately now ceased publication.

Ghost hunters are a rare breed, and the qualifications for joining this elite band are stringent. One has to be incurably eccentric – or even better, clinically insane – and possess an ability to see the world through frighteningly heterodox eyes. If there's even only one person on the planet who would describe you as 'normal' – we ghost hunters detest that word – then you're automatically disqualified. Good ghost hunters need to cloak themselves in a mantle of strangeness that both intrigues and disturbs 'normal' folk, and we're very, very good at it. In short, the world of ghost hunting holds no place for people who are, to coin a phrase, 'cardboard cut-outs'. Diana, like all other real experts in the field, has a larger-than-life personality. She can also put together a cogent argument – or a witty retort – faster than Buffalo Bill Cody could draw a Colt 45.

But let's get serious for a minute. Although ghost hunters benefit from having a good sense of humor and a talent for self-deprecation, one should not assume that they treat their chosen craft lightly. I know from personal experience that Diana takes both ghosts and the hunting of them very seriously indeed. I once took part in a 'celebrity ghost hunt' at a local castle to raise money for a deserving charity (you can find details of this investigation in the section *Face of the Keep*). Diana was there, and deserved to be. Without going into detail, I'll just say this; something happened that night that made the color drain from the faces of several veteran researchers. Their fear was palpable. Diana, for her part, remained perfectly calm. Ever the professional, she kept her head while others were doing their level best not to lose theirs. I really admired her for that.

Books on ghost hunting (I've written a few myself) are usually filled with accounts of white ladies, headless horsemen and spectral nuns. It's about time someone penned something refreshingly different, and Diana has. This book contains a raft of good ghost tales, to be sure, but it's also filled with practical advice and – I like this bit – wry observations and recollections drawn from her personal diaries.

Diana Jarvis has mixed with the Great and the Good during her career, but always kept her feet planted firmly upon the ground. Her earthy humor and disarming candor are endearing, and I suspect have colored this book in a unique way. If you want to know what the world of ghost hunting is really like – as opposed to the tosh one often sees on TV – then you'll not be disappointed with this volume.

Diana Jarvis is a gifted psychic and a good ghost hunter. I have much to thank her for, and feel honored by the opportunity to write this foreword for *Shadows in the Night: Memoirs of a Ghost Hunter*. It provides a unique insight into a decidedly strange profession – and has the good fortune to be penned by one of its most knowledgeable experts and fascinating personalities.

Michael J. Hallowell – columnist, paranormal investigator and author of *Christmas Ghost Stories*.

Chapter 1
Introduction

'Dying is a very dull, dreary affair. And my advice to you is to have nothing whatever to do with it.'
W Somerset Maugham, playwright and novelist, 1874–1965

I am a ghost hunter.

Perhaps this sounds grand to you? If so, you obviously have not experienced the joys of spending a large proportion of your normal sleeping hours awake in cold, dark, damp and unsavory places. Attempting to communicate with the spirits of the dead invariably leads a ghost hunter to places a 'normal' person would not set foot in. Ghost hunting is not glamorous at all; it is cold, dark, damp and unsavory and you will probably have to visit more 'haunted' buildings than there are stories about them, before you'll have a really paranormal experience, let alone a warm one.

As a ghost hunter, I'm not alone. Twenty years ago, I certainly would have been. Any others 'like me' would have been well and truly hidden from public view and any ghost hunter openly admitting to their 'strange' hobby would have been ridiculed and avoided. These days, however, ghost hunters are two a penny.

Although you may not know it, people all around the world go 'spook crazy' every weekend. Thousands of men and women belonging to hundreds of paranormal groups pack flight cases with an assortment of paraphernalia: EMF (ElectroMagnetic

Frequency) meters; digital thermometers; digital camcorders; digital cameras; torches; spare batteries; cotton; pens; notepads; chewing gum; mobile phones...the list goes on. Then they traipse along to whatever house, bar, stately home, castle or shack they have managed to persuade to host them for the night - and get on and do their thing.

Their 'thing' will mean taking copious notes; recording measurements; fiddling with electronic gizmos and producing photographs galore. They may also use mediumistic skills to attempt to communicate with any resident spirits. Then they'll get extremely cold, extremely fed up and wish they were in a warm bar somewhere. However, they will stick to their mission like scandal to a politician and they'll work right through the night...continuing with the same tasks and wishing they were in a bar some more. Nothing much will happen and, just to make matters worse, nothing much will happen virtually every time they do this. The thing is...they will keep doing it.

If you thought that all ghost hunts included at least one exceptional experience, then it's time to put the record straight. If you can't see why anyone would want to stay up all night and discover nothing at all, then I shall reveal why so many ghost hunters will put themselves through this. Their hour after hour of painstaking measuring, recording and sitting around in the cold trying to stay awake has a purpose; despite the fact that it may currently be lost on you. Whilst their television counterparts appear to be experiencing the most amazing phenomena all the time, the average ghost hunter is probably shivering somewhere and taking their umpteenth temperature reading.

Why would they do this? The reason is simple. One night something *will* happen. One night, after weeks, months or years, something quite inexplicable will occur and all those cold and lonely hours will be worth it. It won't be something they see on television or read in a book – it will have happened to *them*. When it does, the ghost hunter will be elevated to the dizzy heights of 'witness' to a paranormal incident, and will be able to regale their friends with the experience forever (or until their friends disperse, whichever comes sooner). More importantly they will have been there themselves, experienced for themselves, and will know what it feels like to come face-to-face with the paranormal. They may even write a book about what happened to them: as many have done before me, and no doubt, many will after. More importantly, they will also, quite possibly, have formulated some kind of answer to the age-old enigma: 'Is there really life after death?'

It is normal for the human psyche to seek something 'more'; something that can't be experienced by the five senses. We all reach a time in our lives when we find ourselves asking: 'Why are we here?'; 'Is there a God?'; 'What happens when we die?' and 'Why don't shoe shops open 24 hours?' As science cannot give us definitive answers to these questions, we will try to find our own answers, because they are so important to us and critical to our spiritual growth. We may not feel we are spiritual, but even if we've reached the conclusion that there is no life after death, we have still considered the other possibilities first. Even the moral codes by which we live our lives are derived from our own spiritual leanings. One does not have to believe in a god or goddess to be a good person, but if we are 'good' then we are so for a reason. Each one of us will die, and each one of us will have to consider the consequences we may suffer (if any) once we have shuffled off this mortal coil. Death is still very much a mystery to humankind, yet it is as much a part of life as shoes are. So we search for answers every day, often without knowing we are doing so. It is usually the case that the only answers that ever mean anything to us are those we define for ourselves.

The paranormal is big business. It has crept into all areas of society and it is no longer odd for someone to have an open discussion about the existence of ghosts. These discussions, and the explorations that follow, are now commonplace – and they are likely to remain so for a very long time. The paranormal has always been a part of our lives, but it is only now, with the explosion of programs covering paranormal topics, that the subject has come out of the closet – skeleton and all.

As Editor of *Vision* magazine, I always had a large mailbag of letters from people who wanted to take their EMF meter in their hand and hike off to their local bar to see what spirits were around after closing. I have explained to them, as I have just explained to you, exactly how cold, boring and tiring a ghost hunt is and I have also illustrated the slim chances of any real experience. I have reminded them that not every orb photographed is paranormal in origin (very few are, in fact), and that they will need to keep a clear head and check frequently to make sure that what they *think* they are seeing is what is actually there. Many times, what they will see is what they most *want* to see, and it is an easy illusion to be taken in by.

Invariably, my advice does not put off these investigator wannabes, though. I am still asked the same question: 'How can I become a ghost hunter?' and I still give the same answer now as I did then. I can point out a number of universities and internet organizations that will give a qualification in the study of the paranormal (unlikely to help much), but there is little else I can do. If *you* want to be a ghost hunter, you have to just 'be' one. Much of this consists of being in the right place at the right time and being determined enough to carry on, even when cold and tired.

The purpose of this book is not to convince you about anything, nor is it intended to be a handbook on the techniques that one can use to connect with the 'Other Side'. It is, from my perspective, a true rendition of many of the more bizarre experiences that I have had.

I have obtained eye-witness accounts to support my stories whenever I have been able, but in some cases I have simply lost touch with my co-investigators of the time. If I've been able to get another perspective, it's been included. I have changed some names to protect those concerned from exposure, but other than that, the accounts herein are accurate from my point of view. Where names have been substituted I have italicized the name. I have also given you some information on how a ghost hunt is organized; what types of equipment are usually used and how to deal with different types of haunting. In some cases I have included my own theories for them, but the final decision on whether there is something 'out there' will always be down to you.

I do hope that in some small way, my experiences may broaden your horizons and may bring you a bit closer to reaching your own answers to both the beginning and the 'end' of the rich tapestry that is life. Maybe, when you've read this, you'll realize that you really *are* mad, and still want to be a ghost hunter after all. If so, I wish you warmth, light, phenomena...and a decent beer afterwards.

Happy Hunting

Diana Jarvis

www.dianajarvis.info

'I think a Person who is thus terrified with the Imagination of Ghosts and Spectres much more reasonable, than one who contrary to the Reports of all Historians sacred and profane, ancient and modern, and to the Traditions of all Nations, thinks the Appearance of Spirits fabulous and groundless.'
Joseph Addison, *The Spectator,* 1711

Chapter 2
What is a Ghost?

'Immortality. I notice that as soon as writers broach this question
they begin to quote. I hate quotation. Tell me what you know.'
Ralph Waldo Emerson, philosopher and poet, 1803–1882

The Concise Oxford English Dictionary defines a ghost as 'the soul of a dead person in Hades etc. appearing to the living.' It is *a* definition, but I don't think that it covers the diversity of experiences that people have had with spirits. It also implies that ghosts exist and live in a state of torment. I'm sure that you will have guessed that I believe in ghosts; however, my belief is not proof. In my humble opinion, no-one will ever be able to conclusively prove or disprove the existence of ghosts. They will only be able to disprove some experiences.

What makes proof ever more difficult is the diversity I've mentioned. When you hear the word 'ghost', what do you think of? Do you see a white sheet with eye-holes and hear 'Boo!'? Do you imagine a floating white lady? Perhaps you think of a brooding presence that you can only see as a black shadow out of the corner of your eye? People have so many different ideas of what ghosts are that ghost hunters have classified different types based on their own experiences as well as ghosts that appear in famous ghost tales.

Non-Sentient Ghosts

From my many conversations with non-ghost hunters, I have formed the opinion that most people would assume that a ghost is the soul or spirit of a human being that has died, but has returned or stayed on earth for one of many possible reasons. They tend to think of ghosts in much the same way as the dictionary describes them. However, not all 'ghosts' behave in a manner which fits this idea. Some ghosts do not seem to be aware that they are dead and some don't seem to be human at all! These types of ghosts I refer to as *non-sentient*.

The Poltergeist

Most people have heard the term 'Poltergeist'. Poltergeist comes from the German *poltern* meaning 'noisy' and *geist* meaning 'ghost'. It's a good name. Poltergeists are invariably noisy: creating knocking noises; throwing things around; moving objects instantaneously (and often loudly); and generally creating a massive disturbance.

One famous Poltergeist case is that of the Rosenheim Poltergeist. In 1967, a legal firm was turned upside down by the antics of a poltergeist in their company. It disrupted the electricity and the telephones (this phenomenon is common in other ghost types), moved pictures and lamps and made strange 'static' noises. The problem was so severe that two physicists from the *Max Planck Institute* were called in to find the cause. Other than discovering that the activity seemed to revolve around a legal secretary called Annemarie Schneider, they could not find any rational or scientific explanation for the goings-on. The case became so well-known that journalists, and even the police, attempted to prove fraud. All failed. When Annemarie finally left the company the poltergeist followed her. Eventually all phenomena ceased and never returned.

One of the physicists, Friedbert Karger, was quoted as saying 'These experiments were really a challenge to physics. What we saw in the Rosenheim case could be 100 per cent shown not to be explainable by known physics.'

Poltergeists are often linked to pubescent children, in particular girls. In some cases it has been shown that the phenomena were simply the children seeking attention and faking things; in some cases though – as above – they have yet to be scientifically explained.

Poltergeists can vary in their attitude: some seem mischievous, some helpful and some are downright nasty!

The Replay

Sometimes referred to as a *residual haunting*, the Replay is exactly what is suggested by its name. This type of ghost is more like a video recording. The witness sees a scene from the past like a movie; any people in it do not respond to the witness, and they go about their daily 'lives' or simply repeat the same tasks over and over again. There is no interaction between ghost and witness at all, other than the witness's ability to see the scene.

One of the most famous replays is that of the Treasurer's House soldiers. Treasurer's House is a beautiful mansion right in the heart of York, UK. In 1953 an apprentice plumber, Harry Martindale, was working on a new central heating system in the bowels of the building. As he labored away, he heard the sound of a horn. He assumed that it came from outside and didn't think much more of it. However, the sound continued and appeared to be coming closer and closer to him. Harry says:

'In the central cellar floor there'd been excavated the original Roman road: I didn't know it had been; I was told later. Someone had been in there and had laid the road out and gone down about 18 inches to the bottom of it, and they'd laid it out in sections of different types of stone. It would've been about 6 feet in diameter. I had to borrow a ladder because I had to knock a hole through the ceiling.'

'I was all alone one day banging away at this ceiling with this hammer and chisel and I kept having to go and get extensions. I came down here the following day to continue to knock the hole through the ceiling. Just before lunchtime I started to hear the sound of musical notes, no tune, just a blaring of a musical note and I thought 'that's unusual' because I was out of the way and the nearest place was the boiler house. Then I realized it was getting louder and louder and at the same time I realized that it was coming from the wall that I was leaning on with the ladder. I just glanced down because something moved and in line with my waist on the right-hand side here I saw a helmet, the top of a helmet come out of the wall.'

Needless to say, Harry was shocked by the helmet and the soldier underneath it – and Harry fell right off his ladder in surprise. As he lay on the floor, unable to do anything, he watched a Roman solider appear, followed by another on a horse. The rider appeared to be a Roman solider from the clothes he was wearing; but his apparel was tatty and he seemed to be completely woebegone. The scene continued to play out and the horse and rider were followed by several more soldiers, all dressed in rough, dirty green tunics and plumed helmets. They were carrying swords, spears and shields. They all looked thoroughly miserable and worn out. Harry watched them march by, in the direction of York Minster. He noticed that they appeared to be marching on their knees; but when they reached the center of the room, where some of the floor had been excavated, he could see that they were actually walking on a different level – that of the old Roman road that was under the surface of the cellar.

Harry finally managed to gather himself together and left the cellar as quickly as possible. He met up with the curator of the house as he was leaving. The curator took one look at his face and said 'You've seen the Roman soldiers, haven't you?' Needless to say, Harry was not the first to see them, but the detail he gave about the scene was impressive. When people think of Roman soldiers, they tend to think of men in shiny, immaculate uniforms; standing proud and ready for battle. Harry's description of their attire and demeanor as well as their physical size and appearance was contrary to what historians at the time believed to be accurate. However, many years later, it turned out that all Harry had said was correct. He had described a group of soldiers that came from the 'Lost' Ninth Legion – unknown at the time of his sighting.

At no time during Harry's experience did the soldiers seem to be aware of his presence at all and they did not interact with him. They were also clearly unaware of their surroundings – they were walking on a road that had been built over for centuries. This is typical of a replay.

I have had the pleasure of interviewing Harry about his experience. He is intelligent, lucid and thoroughly nice. I believe him.

The Stone Tape Theory

There is a theory for how this type of phenomenon may occur and – believe it or not – the theory is based on a television play which was broadcast on a UK terrestrial station in 1972. The story centers on a team of scientists who move into a new research facility, which has been set up in a Victorian mansion. Needless to say, the mansion is haunted and they learn over a period of time that the haunting is a replay: a recording of a traumatic past event that has been held in the very stone of the building. This discovery leads them to believe they may have uncovered a new recording medium and they attempt to learn how the 'stone tape' manages to hold this information. Not surprisingly, their attempts fail and they only manage to release a more malevolent force.

The Stone Tape Theory suggests that buildings and materials are able to absorb and hold a form of energy, which is then released during times of extreme emotional stress (both positive and negative). The energy can be stored for any amount of time and is triggered by a witness that has the right psychological make-up, is in the correct emotional state and is present during certain atmospheric conditions. The replay is not always as detailed as Harry's and could be something as simple as a voice or footsteps. Of course, we have no scientific proof for The Stone Tape Theory, but we do know that substances such as quartz have the ability to hold electricity. Many old houses have quartz as a component of the stones that make them up.

Universal Memory

The other theory for replays is that of universal memory. This theory states that memories are stored in the patterns of life and that there is a universal memory source that lies outside the human body. This source can be accessed by people in the right frame of mind and the right emotional state.

Anniversary Ghosts

These are spirits that appear only at a certain time and place, hence the name 'Anniversary Ghost'. They are very similar to replays, in that they do not appear to interact with witnesses at all, they simply re-enact a certain event.

The *Palatine Light* is a ghost ship that is said to appear off Block Island (near Rhode Island) in New England, USA, between Christmas and New Year. It bursts into flames and sinks and is reputed to be a harbinger of bad weather. There are several different stories about what happened to the real ship. The most widely accepted is that a Dutch ship, which was carrying immigrants to Philadelphia, hit a storm and the crew mutinied; robbing the passengers and leaving the ship to run aground, where it was looted by wreckers. The wreckers set the ship on fire and the tide carried it back out to sea, with some remaining passengers on board. It is said the screams can still be heard as the ship sinks.

Sentient Ghosts

Sentient Ghosts are the most commonly reported. However, even these types of ghost vary. A 'Standard Apparition' is probably the most familiar type of ghost. This can be a fully manifested human figure, or animal figure; but there are also Orbs, Vortexes, Ectoplasm and Shadows. Even this list is not definitive.

Orbs

These are the most common type of apparition, probably because of the ease of mistaking insects, pollen, moisture or dust motes as being something of paranormal origin. Orbs are glowing spherical objects, usually white in color (but not always). They can be seen by the naked eye on occasion, but they are more often caught on photographic media. Identifying a 'genuine' orb from something more mundane is notoriously difficult. Orbs appear to react to their surroundings or, at the very least witnesses – their trajectory can vary in ways that imply there is some sentience. Orbs are said to be the first of the four stages to full manifestation.

Vortexes

These strange phenomena appear as tornado-like swirls and are most often caught on photographic media. On the rare occasion that they are seen, they appear to be made up of hundreds of orbs and seem to exhibit a kind sentience in the way that they move. Vortexes are said to be the second stage towards total manifestation.

Ectoplasm

Ectoplasm comes from the Greek *ektos* meaning 'outside' and *plasma* meaning 'something molded'. It is a term that was coined by Charles Richet in the 1800s. In those days it was common for alleged mediums to hold séances, often as a party trick. The mediums of the day said that when they were fully connected to the spirit of a dear-departed, this substance would exit their body – usually from the nose or mouth. Gauzy in nature, ectoplasm was alleged to be used by entities to cover their non-physical body and therefore help them manifest.

These days, ectoplasm is the name given to a cloud-like form that is, allegedly, the third stage towards total manifestation. The cloud appears to have a type of sentience and moves in a way unlike a mist or fog would do naturally.

Full Apparition

Full apparitions are a lot more uncommon than the media would have you think. The few cases that are reported of witnesses seeing a full human or animal figure tend to come up time and time again. It is extremely difficult for a spirit to have enough energy to be able to fully manifest and your chances of seeing something as spectacular as a full apparition is, sadly, slim. A full apparition is the final stage of manifestation.

Shadow Apparitions

These types of apparition are also widely reported; but perhaps even more commonly talked about! This is the black shadow that moved across your view or the dark shape you saw just out of the corner of your eye.

Although they are usually associated with peripheral vision; there have been cases of shadow apparitions being recorded on photographic media. Despite the dark and brooding nature of their appearance, they are not always accompanied by a feeling of dread; often the witness reports euphoria. The shadow is usually fully human in shape and exhibits sentience.

Crisis Apparitions

Lt. J J Larkin of the RAF was sitting in his barracks reading a book by the fire. It was half past three in the afternoon. A colleague of his, a Lt. David McConnel came in and spoke to him. Larkin noticed he was wearing his flying uniform but had on a naval cap. McConnel said that he had 'got there all right' and had had a good trip. Larkin left the barracks shortly after; it was then that he found out that Lt. McConnel had been killed in a plane crash at 3:25pm that same day. He had been wearing the same clothes Larkin saw him in when he had 'visited' earlier. He was also wearing a naval cap.

Crisis Apparitions are full manifestations of human form that appear at times of crisis. Sometimes they visit a witness to warn the witness of impending danger. They may also appear at the time of their death in order to pass on some information. They will be dying at the same time that they appear. There is also a *Delayed Crisis Apparition*. This ghost will appear a few hours after their death and re-enact it, or pass on a message.

Doppelgängers

This is one of the most unusual types of apparition and possibly one of the most sinister. *Doppel* comes from the German meaning 'double' and *gänger* meaning 'goer'. The apparition is the ghostly double of a living person that appears either to those who would recognize them, or to their living counterpart. When they appear to others, they are usually warning of illness or danger and when they appear to their living double, they usually warn of imminent death.

The famous poet, Percy Bysshe Shelley, met his own doppelgänger in Italy. It pointed silently to the sea. Shortly after, just before his 30th birthday in 1822, Shelley died in a sailing accident.

There are many more types of ghosts – the list seems as huge as the number of reported sightings. The ones I have included are some of the most common and it is possible you may be lucky enough to encounter something that fits the descriptions I've given, should you go ghost hunting often enough. However, there are many more species of spook: look out for stories of Blue

Boys, Screaming Skulls and Revenants, to name but a few more. If you've got the gist of this chapter, you'll now know that the next time someone says to you 'I've seen a ghost' you'll need to ask them exactly what they mean!

Chapter 3
Why Ghost Hunting?

Ghost Hunting, has, without doubt, become a known and recognized pursuit and the discussion of the reality (or not) of ghosts is a common occurrence. I have watched in fascination as the level of interest in this subject has grown beyond all proportion and I have no doubt that a major contributory factor to the interest in the subject is the production of television programs showing ghost hunters in action. The internet has contributed too: a number of opinions, techniques and eye-witness accounts are instantly available to anyone who might be interested.

No longer are ghosts consigned to mention at Hallowe'en or Christmas only, they are an all-round interest and a marketable commodity. Many small businesses exist that peddle ghost hunting equipment and the chance to take part in ghost hunts. The technology that backs up the science of ghost hunting is improving constantly and more and 'smarter' gadgets appear for sale.

City ghost tours have been popular for decades, but the number of people taking them has jumped markedly. Ghost groups are not a modern phenomenon: London's *The Ghost Club* has been in existence since 1862 and is the oldest of its kind. It has a lot more competition these days, with groups springing up on an almost daily basis, accompanied by websites and blogs to support them.

The fascination for ghosts and their questionable existence is almost imprinted on our DNA. It is perfectly natural to want to believe that we exist after death and the search for proof of this can be comforting, even if no proof is found. However, skeptics and scientists question the methodology of ghost hunters, and probably rightly so. Ghost hunting science is often referred to as pseudoscience, as it does not follow normal methodology as exactly as it should: sometimes because the investigators have a complete lack of understanding of science and sometimes because it is very hard to scientifically study the completely intangible. Usually it is both.

One perfect example of how some ghost hunters allow themselves to believe they are being scientific is the EMF meter, which is now a prerequisite for a 'proper' ghost hunt. I have lost count of the number of times I have heard investigators imply that a high reading on this piece of equipment is an indication of a ghost. May I state for the record it is *not!* EMF stands for Electro Magnetic Field or Electro Magnetic Fluctuation and an EMF meter records just that. It does not tell you if a ghost is present in your location. It tells you if the background electromagnetic field in the room is higher (or lower) than you might expect. It can easily be triggered to go off the scale if the meter is held near a fuse cupboard (yes, I've been fooled by that!); and, as some ghost hunters are incredibly enthusiastic, it can also be triggered by their wild waving of this sensitive piece of equipment.

Joe Nickell is a prominent ghost hunter and historical document consultant; but with the advantage of having a degree of skepticism regarding ghost hunting. He says 'The least likely explanation for any given reading is it is a ghost.' Orbs that show up on photos are often dust or moisture; 'voices' appearing on recorders can be noises on the recorder, and EMF meters can be set off by faulty wiring or cables. There are so many traps a ghost hunter can fall into when they investigate and it takes a very methodical and skeptical investigator to produce data of value.

Now back to the original question this chapter asks: why ghost hunting? There are enough reasons for it becoming popular and I've listed a few; but ghosts have been documented for centuries – so why now? The main reason for the explosion in popularity is prompted, in my opinion, by the accessibility of ghost hunting. Anyone can try it. The equipment needed to take readings is not expensive and is easily located. Most people will have at least one friend who claims to be psychic – or a medium. Allegedly haunted locations are not hard to find and as any publicity is good publicity it can be very good PR for a location to allow in a ghost hunting group. In fact, so popular is the hobby now, many locations charge ghost hunting groups for the privilege.

I believe most people would love to delve a little deeper into whether our soul – the real 'us' inside our corporeal shell – continues after we die. Finally, it is possible to do so in a very active way and no longer will one be shunned for pursuing this interest outside of a religious institution. Ghost stories are part of every culture on the planet and have been so for as long as man has recorded information. Who wouldn't want to be able to tell their very own and very personal ghost story to their child on a cold, wet, stormy night – and be sure from their own experience that there is truth in it?

Mediums

Since the increase in paranormal programming, some celebrity mediums have become household names. Indeed, I have been referred to as a celebrity medium – but I doubt that many of you will have heard of me, despite the recent elevation in my status. However, those mediums that have found their way into daily conversation are faced with the public's insistence that they 'deliver' accurate and amazing information *every* time they work. It's a lot of pressure and is almost impossible to maintain. The problem with this pressure is that some mediums become tempted to *ensure* their public is not disappointed. There is also the requirement for a television program (or any media piece) to have entertainment value; so a medium that cannot pick up anything that night is not going to be employed again.

I am not trying to turn you away from your favorite figures or suggest improper behavior. I am pointing out the fact that any program you watch; any radio show you hear or any book you read will have only the best bits in it and the star of the show will be under pressure to deliver those bits. That includes this book too, but the difference between this book and some of the programs that you see is that the events I have described didn't all happen on one night.

Skeptics

Contrary to what you might believe, a skeptic may be just as keen to see if there is life hereafter as a medium is. Skeptics are often part of ghost investigations and their refreshing, down-to-earth approach – as well as their disinclination to accept everything as paranormal – keeps believers' feet on the ground. The popularity of ghost investigation has not just increased the celebrity status of some mediums and paranormal investigators: it has also seen the development of the professional skeptic. Although they do not have the same type of followers at celebrity mediums do, they are called upon at every opportunity to play devil's advocate to any ghostly claims – and rightly so. However, they too are subject to the problem of celebrity: they too must deliver their opposing response to any claims of ghostly activity…every time.

Celebrity

Celebrity can be a problem. The trouble with it is: the more one is courted by fame, the more one is inclined to start to return the compliment. This means that in some cases, fame has got in the way of the ability to be objective. I am scared of anything that goes bump in the night, but I am even more wary of becoming so caught up in media attention that I lose my ability to see what is really in front of me. Although celebrity and media exposure has had the effect of bringing ghost hunting to the attention of the masses, it has also delivered information in a way that makes the public swallow it whole. I am hoping that if you are reading this book you will not buy into what is put in front of you without question. This book is meant to be the subject of debate as well as being a collection of very unusual ghost stories that I hope are an interesting read. This doesn't mean they are not true; I was there and I know they are. However, *you* don't. Enjoy them and then go out and find your own experiences so you *know* for yourself.

Whatever 'side' you take on whether ghosts exist or not; there is some value in ghost hunting. Even if your science is questionable, your medium is less than accurate and your ghost hunt is very short on results, you will find out more about yourself and your beliefs and values than you can imagine. You will end up asking yourself questions you thought you had answered long ago and you will perhaps find your answer has changed. You will know – from your *own* experience – what is really out there (or at least what you think is really out there). Most of all you will get out in the fresh air; meet other people and be part of something that stimulates interest and debate. Instead of watching ghosts hunts on television and commenting 'that must be very interesting to do' you can say 'I did that!'

Chapter 4
Ghost Hunting Techniques

'It is sometimes important for science to know how to forget the things she is surest of.'
Jean Rostand, French Historian and Biologist, 1894–1977

The majority of the experiences in this book happened during ghost investigations. As I have intimated earlier, ghost investigations are often very, very boring. For this reason, I have concentrated on highlighting the most unusual experiences I've had during investigations – the best bits – rather than the whole event. However, to give you some idea of what a full ghost investigation entails, I thought it was only right to include a chapter on some of the methodology used by ghost hunters.

What type of ghost hunter are you?
As well as different types of equipment, ghost investigation also requires different types of investigator. Although some ghost hunting groups concentrate only on one aspect of a ghost investigation, the majority attempt to use both psychic and scientific methods to determine if there is anything paranormal present. The terms I've used are ones that I've come across; but there really isn't anything definitive. Every ghost group will give out their own titles and tasks to attendees.

Chief Investigator

This person runs the show. They decide on the agenda for the night and they keep an eye on everything that is going on. They are usually responsible for Health and Safety and risk assessments, too.

Science Investigator

Science Investigators use scientific methodology and record data during the investigation. They will usually collate data from all the paranormal investigators as well as provide a report.

Paranormal Investigator

This is a catch-all term for anyone who is taking an active part in an investigation. It also covers those members of the team who work with the science investigator to gather data, but are happy to perform other tasks, such as taking photographs and dowsing.

Investigative Medium

There may be one or more of these on the team during investigations, although some teams prefer not to work with mediums at all. The medium attempts to use psychic methods to connect with any resident spirits. They will then pass on any information they glean; including – but not limited to – a description of the spirit, historical details and a reason why the spirit is there. In most cases any information gathered from the investigative medium is very subjective, but historical details can be put to the test to some degree. However, it is never entirely possible to preclude the chance that the medium has read up on the building and its alleged spirits. In some cases, though, the information the medium provides *does* give a degree of provenance that cannot be explained away by previous research.

Ghost Hunting Equipment

Ghost hunters love gadgets. These vary from something as simple as a notebook and pencil to some recording equipment that is so high tech, you might wonder if it's been stolen from NASA. For the purposes of this list, I've included the pieces of equipment used most often.

EMF (ElectroMagnetic Field or ElectroMagnetic Fluctuation) meter

EMF meters are one of the most popular pieces of kit in a ghost hunter's case. I believe that their popularity can be ascribed mostly to their regular appearances during ghost investigation TV series. They look good, they sound good and they make you think that you're doing something really scientific.

EMF meters detect levels of electromagnetic fluctuation, and are measured in *milligauss*. For this reason, they are sometimes referred to as 'gauss meters'. Electrical equipment creates an electrical field and most places will have background levels of these fields present. The EMF meter detects the strength of this field and can detect unusual levels.

There is a theory that in order for a ghost to manifest, a great deal of energy is required. The obvious place for a spirit to draw energy from is the electromagnetic field in a building, and that is why the EMF meter is used. Dramatic fluctuations and very high readings are unusual and may support any other anomalous readings taken in the same area. An EMF meter will not prove a ghost is present. Nothing will.

Electricity sources can create phenomena all by themselves, though. It is extremely common for electrical equipment to fail during a ghost hunt – especially if the place seems to be particularly active. Brand new batteries drain; cameras stop working and laptops close down. Although in many cases there may be a perfectly rational explanation for these sudden failures, there are still occasions where it is easier to believe a spirit is playing with the electricity than it is to believe that something has failed! I would highly recommend that investigators take more batteries than they could possibly need. Just in case.

Digital Camera

Every ghost investigation I've attended has had at least one person sporting a digital camera. They are hugely popular because they give instant results and can be studied at length after the event, too. Digital cameras are particularly adept at picking up orbs and during my time as a ghost investigator I have noticed that some digital cameras seem to be better at this than others; and that they are better than others *consistently*. I have not found any particular reason for this; the make, model or quality does not seem to be the key factor. I have to admit I am very skeptical of orbs picked up on digital cameras, although I have seen a few that I find very hard to explain scientifically. When taking photos for ghost investigations it is always a good idea to take a few shots in succession so that you can see if the object is travelling – or when it appears and disappears.

SLR Cameras

The Single Lens Reflex camera, or SLR camera, is not as popular as a digital camera for ghost investigations, which is a shame. An SLR camera can be very handy to have. Using traditional film, SLRs are much less sensitive to orbs, so picking one up on film is of great interest – especially as it's not possible to use a graphics program on a hard copy picture to fake an orb (unless you scan it). However, film means development. Very often, ghostly images or other phenomena are simply the product of poor developing practices or old film.

Night Shot (Infrared / Zero Lux) Camcorders

Many camcorders come with a night shot option; which means the camera can use *infrared* or *zero lux* capability. Both zero lux and infrared camcorders produce similar results, but in different ways.

Infrared 'sees' at a range above the visible spectrum and most camcorders that work on infrared actually operate just below it – at a level called near-infrared (NIR).

Lux is Latin for light, so it's clear what zero lux means. Except that it doesn't. Zero Lux cameras require some light, but pitch dark is never complete dark. There is always some light present however dark it may seem. Zero Lux camcorders take the small amount of light present in the dark and spread it around, so that it is possible to 'see'. With the addition of a tripod, a zero lux camcorder can monitor and record a room when you can't be there yourself. Footage can be analyzed at a later date, too.

Digital Thermometers

As well as phenomena connected with electricity; ghosts are also said to affect the temperature surrounding them, so temperature readings are taken during most ghost investigations. The commonest misconception is that a spirit will always turn the air icy cold as it draws the heat to help itself manifest. I have found that temperature variations both down and up can be an indication of paranormal activity and not every spirit that has come through to me has made me shiver. Infrared digital thermometers are the most popular type used during investigations.

Motion Sensors

These are used as a way of monitoring a room that will not be entered at all during the investigation and is left secure. A motion sensor will detect any movement within a certain range of the sensor. So long as the investigators have been very careful to make sure that nothing can enter the room (not even an insect), they can be pretty sure that they will have a paranormal occurrence, should the sensor go off. They will not have proof of a ghost, but they will have 'evidence'.

Dowsing Rods and Pendulums

These pieces of equipment are not scientific at all, but are used by both mediums and investigators alike, as they are so simple to use.

Dowsing rods are two lengths of metal that are been bent at right angles to form an 'L' shape. A forked twig (traditionally hazel) can also be used. The rods are held with the small piece in the fist and the long piece out in front – one in each hand. Dowsing has been used for centuries as a method to find water, but it is also useful as a means of picking up energy lines or areas of paranormal activity. The dowser simply 'thinks' what they want to find and the rods indicate when an area fitting the description has been found. The rods usually cross to indicate a positive result, but not always. The results from dowsing rods are often subjective, but when tied in with other readings can add to a body of 'evidence'. They are also useful to determine the best places to lock-off camcorders.

Pendulums are shaped very similarly to plumb-bobs on a plumb-line and come in a variety of materials: everything from wood to semi-precious stones. They indicate activity in much the same way as the dowsing rods; the difference being that results are indicated by the way they swing.

Dictation Devices

Dictation devices are popular tools for a number of reasons. They save making lots of illegible notes because you can record data and thoughts in the dark without any fear of being unable to read them afterwards. They are also used to produce EVPs.

I have elaborated on EVPs later in the book, but in short, EVP means *Electronic Voice Phenomena*. It has been discovered that occasionally voices appear on a recording when there was no noise being made or heard at the time of that recording. Before recorders became digital; many of these noises could be credited to stretched or old tape. With digital recorders, these problems disappear, but it is still possible to pick up the noise of the recorder on the recording.

Walkie-Talkies

Two-way radios or walkie-talkies are often used for Health and Safety reasons, as well as to ensure that all attendees can be located, should they be needed. They are cheaper to use than cell phones and cause less disruption to an investigation.

Notepads and Pens

Every investigator should have a notepad and pen; it is amazing how many forget these most basic pieces of equipment. These are used for everything from recording data to drawing impressions of spirits.

Trigger Objects

A trigger object is used to determine if there has been any movement in a locked-off room. Cheaper than a motion sensor, but much more 'local' with its results, the object usually consists of something that could be easily identified by people across the ages. Popular trigger objects are crosses, coins and keys.

The object is placed on a plain piece of paper that is bigger than the object; where it is held down and very carefully drawn around. Then it's left inside its outline and the room is locked. At least two people are present for this set-up (to guarantee no cheating) and at least two people will check on it at any given time. If the object moves outside of the outline, the result is said to be paranormal.

Ouija Boards

These pieces of equipment have the most fearsome reputation. They consist of a board with the alphabet; the numbers 0–9 and the words 'Hello', 'Goodbye', 'Yes' and 'No' on them. They usually come with an addition called a planchette, which is a small flat triangular board, often on castors. The investigators who wish to take part will put one finger on the planchette and ask for the spirits to speak to them using the board.

Everyone has their own opinions on the danger (or not) of the Ouija Board. My personal opinion is that if you don't know what you are doing – if you are at all unsure – keep away from them. They very rarely offer much in the way of any kind of evidence. I have used them, I haven't had a really negative experience and I can't honestly say that I consider them to be valuable additions to an investigation. They can be 'interesting' and that's about it.

The Séance

Most investigations will include a séance. The séance has almost as many detractors as the Ouija board and it must be borne in mind that anything received in a séance is going to be subjective. I have attended and conducted many, many séances.

As with the Ouija board, my advice to you is; if you are unsure, don't do it. Séances should really have at least one medium present and everyone in the room should know how to psychically protect themselves. Don't ask 'Is anybody there?' I believe this is very much the same as visiting the very worst neighborhood you can think of and asking if anyone wants to come to visit you. Be specific and ask for resident spirits to come through – or you are likely to get the flotsam and jetsam of the universe knocking on your door. Ask in the name of the 'Higher Good', or do the sensible thing and avoid it entirely unless you are with people who really know what they are doing.

Chocolate

Chocolate is a prerequisite for every investigation I have attended. Believe it or not, I can support the need for it. Bear in mind these points about a typical night:

- You are not going to get to sleep at all;

- You will probably be very cold and this will make you feel sluggish;

- You will need your wits about you;

- You may get quite miserable after several hours.

Chocolate is the original 'fast food'. Yes, in quantities it *is* bad for your health. However, if you need a quick energy boost and want to feel good, chocolate can provide both of these things in the cheapest and most pleasurable form. Besides, it's not all bad. Dark chocolate benefits the circulatory system and a report by the *British Broadcasting Corporation* showed that melting chocolate in the mouth produces an increase in brain activity and increases the heart rate to a level higher than that associated with passionate kissing. The results last four times longer, too.

Seriously, though: make sure you have hot drinks and snacks with you on your investigation. Working all night long is not for everyone, but everyone will need to make sure they keep hydrated and have calorific reserves to draw upon.

Gathering Data
At the very start of an investigation, the team will usually choose one location to act as a base camp and work from there. The team will be apportioned their roles and a schedule of tasks will be drawn up – with regular breaks and check-ins.

Baseline Tests
The first task is usually a tour of the building with everyone taking part. This is to make sure that everyone knows the layout; that all the rooms have been given names to make it easy to understand data, and also to ensure that fire exits and meet-up

points have been determined. Another reason for the tour is so that baseline tests can be performed. The baseline test is crucial, as it determines 'normal' readings on all the equipment before the investigation starts properly. Finally, the tour gives the medium the chance to say which areas he or she believes will be the most active. Dowsing rods and pendulums can be used at this point too.

The investigation then continues, with readings being taken at regular intervals and the medium being escorted to key locations and their findings being recorded. EVPs may be taken and any of the other equipment may be used at any point the investigators see fit, providing the science investigator deems this use to be appropriate. Most investigations include at least once séance, and usually conclude with one.

The equipment and methods in this chapter are based on my own experiences and may give you an idea of how an investigation is conducted. Each investigation will vary and each ghost investigation group will have their own way of doing things. I am not claiming that my way is the only right and definitive way; it is simply a way that works for me.

'By three methods we may learn wisdom: first, by reflection, which is noblest; second, by imitation, which is easiest; and third, by experiences, which is the most bitter.'
Confucius, Chinese philosopher and political theorist, 551–479BC

Chapter 5
Celebrity Ghosts

'While yet a boy I sought for ghosts, and sped
Through many a listening chamber, cave and ruin,
And starlight wood, with fearful steps pursuing
Hopes of high talk with the departed dead.'
Percy Bysshe Shelley, *Hymn to Intellectual Beauty*

Contrary to popular belief, it is not usual for the spirits of celebrities and famous historical figures to be seen or communicated with on a regular basis, much as we'd like to think so. If these well-known figures are seen at all, it tends to be in one location only. They are definitely not known for 'following' a particular person and attempting to communicate with them at every available opportunity. Generally speaking, spectral celebrities stick to one place to haunt and are rarely seen there – only occasionally will they grace some poor unsuspecting ghost hunter with their presence.

There are exceptions of course. Some spirits seem to be able to get around a number of locations, if everything read were to be believed. You may be surprised to find that Anne Boleyn is alleged to appear in several locations in the UK. Blickling Hall, Norfolk; Hever Castle, Kent; Hampton Court, Surrey and the Tower of London are supposed to be regular haunts of her spirit. I'm not sure that I believe one tiny Tudor lady can manage to be so tied to so many places, and I don't know of any one person that has communicated with her in more than one of these locations. Her shade may well be walking all of these hallowed corridors for all I know, but I don't understand how (or why) it would do so. In general, celebrity ghosts do exist, but they are a rare treat, not a common occurrence. Stories of them are much more common than they are.

The same cannot be said for a couple of ghostly celebrities that have come into, and out of, my life. These characters have positively stalked me, and have taken the same attitude towards some of my friends, too. I don't know why.

- Perhaps these particular ghosts were just *so* nasty in their life that they carried over their guilt to the afterlife.

- Maybe they decided that they would be better off staying around the earth plane to pester anyone they thought may be worth the effort...instead of showing some decency and passing over to potential divine retribution.

- Perhaps they are able to make themselves felt and can travel around more easily *because* they were unpleasant in life, I am not sure.

However, I *am* sure that two malevolent specters have plagued me in my past and that I don't want to ever experience either of them again. I don't know why they were so persistent. Perhaps when you have read about them you may think you know why. If so, do write to the publishers and tell me!

Bad, Bad Lord de Soulis

'You can discover what your enemy fears most by observing the means he uses to frighten you.'
Eric Hoffer, social writer and philosopher, 1902–1983

Lord William de Soulis was a very bad man. By bad, I don't mean that he didn't wash his hands after going to the lavatory, or that he sneaked into a cinema by the fire exit without paying for his ticket. By bad, I mean *bad*. De Soulis was lord of the Hermitage Castle in Roxburghshire (now the Scottish Borders) from 1318 to 1320, and he also held the Lordship of Kilmarnock. The combination of these two positions gave him considerable power; and this power he used indiscriminately. There are stories that he boiled babies and used their blood in black magick rituals, and that you were probably in danger of experiencing his wrath in a very personal and terminal way if you so much as looked at him sideways. He was truly despised so much and trusted so little, that King Robert the Bruce eventually sanctioned an angry mob to 'execute' him. This decision was made so much easier by the fact that in addition to all his other alleged foul deeds, de Soulis had decided to side with the hated English against the king. However, it seems that in those days even a simple (and one would assume, definitive) decision to have a man killed was subject to *Murphy's Law* (anything that can go wrong, will go wrong) and it took more than one attempt to rid the world of de Soulis.

To be truthful, a mob against de Soulis was not really an even

36

match. De Soulis was a monster of a man in both size and deed and he demonstrated a cruelty that could win awards. When he became the Lord of Hermitage Castle he wasted no time in becoming loathed by all around him. Stories grew of the extent of his vileness (this included – but was not limited to – baby boiling) and the locals started to attribute his ability to be so despicable to an allegiance with a redcap.

Redcaps (sometimes known as *powries* or *dunters*) are best described as ugly, squat and resembling old men – but with the addition of red eyes, taloned hands and large teeth. They are said to inhabit ruined castles, with this belief persisting mainly along the Scottish / English border. They get their name from…wait for it…a trademark red cap. Their red cap is their life. The red comes from bloodstains and the redcap is obliged to kill in order to keep the stains on the cap fresh. If the stains dry, the redcap dies. Needless to say, they were very much feared amongst the inhabitants of the Hermitage Castle area, especially as they were in league with the Devil (affectionately called Clootie). They would kill whatever or whomever they needed in order to keep a fresh supply of bloodstains. They could move very fast in order to catch and kill their prey, despite being weighed down by metal-bound boots and a heavy pikestaff. It is said that the only way to escape a redcap is to quote a passage from the bible at them. If this method is successfully employed, not only will the potential victim escape, but the redcap will lose a tooth.

Without a doubt, the most feared redcap of all was Robin Redcap, and it was this charming creature that de Soulis was alleged to have as his familiar and who helped him to contact the Devil.

At this point it might help you to understand a little about beliefs in the Highlands during this period of time. It is unlikely that many people will give credence to the existence of a murdering goblin in the 21st Century, but de Soulis did not live in the 21st Century. He lived in a time when many such creatures were believed to exist and were blamed for all manner of misfortunes (and occasionally, good luck). Here are just a few of the creatures that were said to inhabit 14th Century Scotland.

> **Black Donald or Clootie:** The Devil. He was believed to roam the earth on a fairly regular basis, causing trouble as he went.
> **Brownies:** Invisible elves reputed to wear brown clothing. They would undertake household tasks in return for a saucer of milk. Upsetting a brownie so that it left the house was considered to be extremely bad luck.
> **Fachen:** A strange creature made of one leg, one arm and one eye.
> **Ghillie Dhu:** A solitary Scottish elf.
> **Kelpie:** A water devil.
> **Selkie:** A supernatural marine creature that took the form of a seal.
> **Shellycoat:** A bogeyman covered in shells that haunted rivers and streams.
> **Sidhe:** The mysterious faerie folk of Ireland and Scotland. Tall, slim and with coal-black eyes, these faeries bear no resemblance whatsoever to the little flower-loving winged folk we usually think about.

Now back to de Soulis! Although he had the ability to call on Robin Redcap to perform foul deeds for him, de Soulis did not always need to call upon a demon to terrorize locals. In 1320 he is said to have kidnapped a woman from under the nose of her father simply because he felt like it. He was already leaving with her for the Hermitage when her father tried to stop him. De Soulis killed the man without hesitation. This deed took long enough for an angry mob to form (there was no television in those days) and after they had witnessed de Soulis' despicable act, they were ready to kill him on the spot. However, one Alexander Armstrong, the Laird of Mangerton, arrived and managed to calm down the crowd as well as convince de Soulis to leave for the Hermitage without the girl. So de Soulis got away.

You would be forgiven for thinking that de Soulis would be grateful for this act of kindness from Armstrong – but you would be wrong. He almost instantaneously developed a hatred for the man; probably because Armstrong had the ability to control the crowd despite being de Soulis' social inferior. So, pretending to befriend Armstrong, de Soulis invited him to a banquet at the Hermitage. When Armstrong arrived, he stabbed him in the back.

By the time de Soulis had done away with Armstrong, the King had already heard more than enough tales of de Soulis' behavior. It is said that the King cried out 'Soulis! Soulis! Go boil him in brew!' It seems that the locals took him at his word and this is the point where the angry mob was reformed – now with the King's blessing – and this time they meant business.

In my opinion, all good stories have an angry mob, but there has to be some justification for local peasants to want to leave their turnips to execute someone. By now you will probably have realized that de Soulis was a very good justification. Living your life as a baby-boiling, maid-kidnapping, murderous Black Magician in league with the Devil has never, in the whole of history, been a way to make friends and influence people. I like to think that our angry mob wielded pitch-forks, spades and flaming torches, but I can't find any evidence to support my mental image.

Now the mob took their responsibilities very seriously (whether they actually had pitch-forks or not) and were not prepared to be talked out of killing de Soulis a second time. They embraced their task with gusto, and some considerable planning. Fearing de Soulis' magick, the mob grabbed him first and asked questions later. They dragged him to a handy stone circle called *Nine Stane Rigg*, where they thought they might have some protection from the evil that they believed oozed out of every pore of his body. In Nine Stane Rigg, they had a cauldron with a fire going underneath and water bubbling in it. They took de Soulis and wrapped him in lead, bound him with a specially constructed chain and then proceeded to boil him vigorously until he was as dead as he could possibly be. With much pomp, ceremony and not a little fear of afterlife retribution, they rid the world of the curse that was de Soulis.

Or did they? Normally, dead means *dead*, and the mob were pretty sure they'd done the deed, as you would be if you'd boiled a man in a cauldron, after putting him in a lead overcoat. But, as you'll see from my confrontations with de Soulis, one can never be too sure that someone is properly dead.

Now you might be thinking that a lead wrap and a boiling cauldron was a lot of trouble for an angry mob to go to, just to kill a man. In my opinion you'd be right, under normal circumstances. However, de Soulis was not just a man, he was a Black Magician. The lead shroud ensured he was weighed down (if witches float, then surely an accomplished black magician would?), and Robin Redcap protected him from harm by steel, so they figured they would be safe with lead. Redcap also gave de Soulis the ability to call on the Devil, but we'll come back to this later.

De Soulis didn't seem to want to die. In life he didn't want to and, in whatever limbo or 'afterlife' he had found himself in once he had shuffled off this mortal coil, he hadn't changed his attitudes or his tenacity to try to control and terrorize people. He had no intention of resting in peace, or in any other state.

I know this from the numerous encounters I've had with his ghost, two of which I'll recount for you here. Why he picked on me and my associates to terrorize I am not sure, although I have some sketchy theories. Whatever the reason, de Soulis didn't like me at all.

Knock Three Times

*'Remember that fear always lurks behind perfectionism.
Confronting your fears and allowing yourself the right to be human
can, paradoxically, make you a far happier and more productive
person.'*
Dr David M Burns, author of health and lifestyle titles

My first encounter with bad Lord de Soulis was at Hermitage
Castle itself.

Hermitage Castle is black, bleak and bare. The land around,
although fine Scottish moorland with the mandatory gorse and
heather, lacks any kind of attraction, as far as I'm concerned. It is
windswept, soulless and cheerless and if you are tired, fed up
and cold, it will inch its way into your mood and suck out the
good bits like marrow from a bone. On this particular day it was
raining hard and blowing a gale, so what good bits were left in
my mood were pretty cold, damp and not too bothered if they
were removed, anyway. They had places they'd rather be.

Five associates and I had piled into my car and had headed
for Chillingham Castle, via Hermitage Castle. We were certainly
a motley crew.

There was John Mason, a good friend to us all. He was a keen
attendee to many vigils, but never really saw anything or felt
anything; he just liked to come along for the ride. He was a
professional photographer, so often took this role when out with
our team. He is a wonderful personality, always fun to have
around – he could be so rude in such a poker-faced way. I was
glad of his company to cheer me up and glad of his skills in case
we experienced anything that could be recorded on film.

On this occasion, we had *Sheila* with us too. This was a rarity
as she did not normally ghost hunt with us. She had been added
to a filming list for Chillingham Castle, where we were
ultimately headed in order to be filmed for a German TV

41

company. This actress and presenter was a very pleasant young lady. With long natural blonde hair, an attractive figure and a friendly personality, she was not well-known as a ghost hunter – but did allege to be psychic and was certainly a believer in the afterlife. She probably would have been good company, but she was far too friendly with *Marcus*, who considered himself an actor, too. Put two actors together and, it seems, they will ignore anyone who isn't an actor and behave as if they aren't there…just in case any attempt is made to steal their limelight. Who exactly would be interested in their limelight in the wilds of the Scottish Borders on a cold, wet day I do not know, but obviously there was the chance it might happen because *Sheila* and *Marcus* were busy ignoring the rest of us for all they were worth.

Marcus is a parapsychologist that I was working with very closely at the time. I shall refrain from writing a diatribe on him in this book. I'll just say he was *very* experienced at ghost hunting, a mine of information on haunted places and very knowledgeable and practiced at parapsychology. However, I must add that he had not acquired the knack of respecting anyone, nor did he seem to understand that it not polite to speak to people as if they were unworthy peasants.

Also with us was *Margie, Marcus's* best friend. She was quite a character and this character was perhaps more defined as she was in her fifties and the rest of us were considerably younger. She relied on *Marcus* for support and direction. Very often she ended up doing things that were not her forte, because *Marcus* encouraged her. Despite that, I liked her.

Then there was me. I was the designated driver for our trip and I was pretty fed up (driving and being fed up seemed to go hand in hand with all my ghost hunting exploits that involved *Marcus*). I was trying to keep my focus on getting us to our destination without getting killed, as I had had very little sleep and I hadn't wanted to go to the Hermitage at all. If some bright spark hadn't suggested this detour, we would have been well on our way to Chillingham Castle.

My car wound its way around the pitted track that led to the castle, a track that broke every Trade Description law by calling itself a road. I had successfully avoided the sheer drop on one side of this 'road', which had ensured that I had stayed awake, focused and terrified. *Marcus* had nodded encouragement while I was driving ('nodded encouragement' is a euphemism for screaming at me if I said I was scared to fall off the edge and didn't want to go any further), which wasn't that welcome as he couldn't drive a car himself.

Finally I had made it to the bit of gravel that was laughingly called the car park. We were all still in one piece so things were going ok, despite the miserable surroundings. We got out of the car and trudged up to the castle through the wind, rain and mud.

Being out of the tourist season the castle was closed and locked, but still accessible around the perimeter. So around we went, looking at the formidable square building, peering through the holes that were supposedly windows and taking in the complete lack of anything redeemable. We even went up to the door and studied the huge, but otherwise unremarkable, knocker. We tried it a few times to make sure there wasn't a little man hiding, waiting to take some entry money from us, but we couldn't get it to move. The wind was whistling up a gale now, and it was raining in a way that only the northern parts of the UK can rain – sheets and sheets of cold water that seem to miss out on clothes and skin entirely and make straight for the bone.

There wasn't a little man, nor was there any budging the knocker. We turned our backs on the Hermitage and started making our way back to my car, which was looking rather lonely and a little nervous. We had only taken a few steps, complaining about a wasted trip as we went, when we heard 'the noise'. Bang! Bang! Bang! Clear as a bell we heard it, but this was not a cheerful church bell praising God and the joys of earthly life. No, this dull monotone was morbid and echoing and it chilled me to the marrow. It was a death-knell if ever I'd heard one (and I hadn't, but I'm sure that if I had, it would have sounded just the same).

We were all astounded at the noise as we could not see any way it was being generated. There was no one for miles. At this point, I am tempted to tell you for the sake of creative prose, that I froze in horror and fear when I heard the banging. However, I think I'll just come right out and say that I was getting dangerously close to needing a change of underwear when the strange and unearthly banging echoed around the Hermitage. Imagine the wind howling; imagine the cold, the rain, the scrubby and bleak landscape and then imagine an imposing dark building towering over you, devoid of human life except yourself and your colleagues. Then imagine a terrible noise with no rational explanation. See? Scary! I don't think my colleagues were faring much better than I was in the 'let's pretend not to be afraid' stakes, but they weren't saying. I was panicking, loudly.

One thing I do make a point of when I am on a ghost investigation, is saying if I'm scared. I don't think it's big or clever to pretend that I'm fine when I'm not; and I think that a little warning of my fragile state of mind means that anyone with me can prepare for:

- A hernia, trying to catch me when I faint;

- My total and complete breakdown into tears and shaking;

- A sudden push as I rush headlong in the opposite direction from whatever it is that is scaring me;

- A punch in the face if they get in my way when I'm running.

I was making it clear that I was scared right now. There was no-one but us in the castle grounds. Because of our position, which allowed us to see for some considerable distance, it was also clear there was no-one around for *miles*. This was not a nice thought, but I was having it, just the same. I'm not keen on visiting places alleged to be haunted by mass-murderers. If they are also cold and wet places without any redeemable features, they just add to my innate fear that something unexpected may hurt me if I'm not somewhere convivial on a bright sunny day. The Hermitage was neither convivial nor sunny. If something was making a noise and I couldn't explain what was doing it, all my senses said that I was in danger and my fight or flight mechanisms busied themselves with trying to figure out how to both function at the same time.

We turned round, naturally, to see where the noise was coming from. One look at the door knocker confirmed that the only thing that could have made a noise like the one we had just heard was hanging from the door – unless the banging was of a paranormal nature. Wishing to be rational and act like the ghost investigators we claimed to be, we went back to the door. We tried, countless times, to replicate the noise by attempting to bang the knocker. It wouldn't move at all.

John took lots of pictures which had wonderful arrays of orbs on them. This is not really surprising as it was raining, and raindrops make wonderful orbs. The others continued to try to figure out where the noise was coming from. *Margie* was looking a bit bemused and *Sheila* and *Marcus* were trying to come up with an explanation while checking their hair. I just carried on being scared.

After our efforts, we waited, allowing the wind to have a go at making the noise. We heard nothing, nothing at all. There was only the wind, the rain, the mud, and five cold, wet, scared individuals who knew in their heart of hearts that they had better leave as quickly possible. We left, still none the wiser about where the noise really came from, and completely sure that it was better for us if we didn't find out.

Unfortunately, one of us got a good lead on what the noise could be, some weeks later. That person was me, but I can assure you I was not happy it was me. As I had offered to write up our trip to Chillingham and our detour to the Hermitage, I did a little research on the castle and its unpleasant shade. In the course of my research I came across de Soulis' *aide de camp*, Robin Redcap, and the piece of information that might explain the (so far) inexplicable noise.

As you will remember, Robin Redcap, de Soulis's handy demonic familiar, had conveyed upon de Soulis the power to call the Devil. The extra piece of information that I discovered in my research is exactly *how* he did this.

He would bang three times on an iron chest!

Folklore, superstition and hearsay, maybe; but to me it was a pretty good description of the noise that I had heard distinctly coming from the completely empty and unattended ruin that was the Hermitage castle. If there was ever a prelude to a run-in with Satan's right-hand man, the banging at the Hermitage gets ten out of ten for being convincing. It also rates highly in the 'this is a warning' stakes...

Cut and Run

'Nothing is easier than to denounce the evildoer; nothing is more difficult than to understand him.'
Fyodor Dostoevsky, Russian writer and essayist, 1821–1881

Many months later, I met up with Rachel Lacy. Known affectionately as York's 'Ghost Finder General', Rachel has been my co-worker and support on many a ghost investigation. Apart from being an exceptionally dedicated paranormal investigator, Rachel has ancestral connections with William de Soulis. This is a fact that might be worth knowing if you fancy trying to analyze why a murderous Scottish specter would continually haunt me. It's hard to see why one spirit would spend so much of his own personal eternity trying to scare the living daylights out of me and my friends, and travel to York to do so, but he did.

York, UK, is definitely worth a visit, whether you are interested in the paranormal or not. It is a beautiful and historical city, so I can see the attraction of York for anyone, living or dead. However, the allure of York has prompted my alternative theory for de Soulis' appearance there – other than that of Rachel's ancestral connection or making the assumption he was out to get me (not a theory I wanted to believe in), I think he may just have fancied tea at the world-famous *Betty's Tearooms* and thought he'd fit in some terrorizing while he was in the area, to maximize his time.

Every year, York holds a ghost festival. Or rather, Rachel Lacy organizes a ghost festival on a shoestring budget, in order to give some of the inhabitants of York the chance to investigate a haunted place with a team of genuine investigators. Rachel always does a sterling job, both for the tourism of York and for the people who attend: at no profit to herself.

This particular year, as part of York's Ghost Festival, there was to be a ghost investigation in York Dungeon. This popular tourist attraction is a place I had spent many a night in, conducting public séances. The 'dungeon' is creepy, haunted and smells, but this just adds to its atmosphere and goes down a storm with the paying public. I liked the staff at the dungeon and always got on really well with its over-worked manager Helen Douglas. However, I can't say I've ever liked the place; more's the pity, as I ended up there so often.

So, on the night of the festival, we formed up as a really mixed bag of die-hard investigators. There was Rachel (whom you've already met), James, *Amanda*, Dru, Angi, Jenny and myself, all ready to help the public have a go at finding out if the place was really haunted, and all experienced investigators. We had had a fantastic turnout of the paying public to help us explore the dungeon and any resident ghosts, so the mediums were each given their own group of would-be investigators to take off to different locations within the building. As well as being labeled 'an investigator and ghost hunter' I am also considered a medium; i.e. someone who communicates with the dead. Because of this alleged ability, I was given my own group.

My group liked to ask questions. They asked about everything, from 'why do you do spend so much of your time looking for ghosts in dark, scary places?' to 'tell us about the spirit that's scaring you?' The latter question came as we started one of the last séances that night in one of the many rooms that make up the rabbit warren of York Dungeon.

I was sensing the spirit of a man, and I didn't like him. Part of me was convinced I'd 'met' him before, and that part was currently reminding me that I should perhaps consider leaving before 'fight and flight' had a dispute, as they so often do. That part was winning its argument over the part that suggested I should really try to find out more about him. It argued that I should do this if not for myself, but for the group that had paid good money to come on this investigation. My sense of responsibility finally won the argument despite the pleas of my natural urges, so I pushed a little harder to try to find out about the spirit, hoping I could relay my findings to the group.

By now, you'll know that the spirit was de Soulis as the start of this chapter does hint at that, and you're not daft. You are probably wondering how I knew it was him. It is going to be very hard to explain this, but I shall try. I am a clairsentient medium; so more than anything else, I rely on how I feel – both emotionally and physically – to determine what spirits are what. I don't get visions very often. Clairsentience is the ability to *feel* the psychic, supernatural and paranormal, clairvoyance is the ability to see it.

I have found that most spirits seem to have a 'signature'. They will make me feel hot or cold in a certain area; will make me feel elated or depressed; or they may even make me want to vomit. De Soulis had a very unique signature, which I'm sure comes as no surprise. I have 'met' a great many spirits in my time, but not many that can list murder, torture, extreme cruelty, a hotline to the Devil and an horrific and complicated death on their résumé.

What de Soulis was doing in York I don't know (still mulling over the *Betty's* idea), but I do know that spirits seemed to travel far and wide to get to York dungeon. The only theory I can come up with, which doesn't involve tea or persecution, is the innumerable Ley Lines that are alleged to cross through York. Ley Lines are various 'imaginary' lines along which certain ancient, man-made structures are thought to have been aligned. Current belief has it that spirits can travel along these lines easily. I'll settle for that as an explanation to give you. Do feel free to come up with your own.

De Soulis was bothering me. I had no doubt in my mind by now that it was he that was haunting me, for I didn't think he was haunting the dungeon. He just turned up periodically to scare me witless, and this time he had picked a public séance to do so. My group pressed me further, so I started to tell them what I knew about him. 'Started' is the operative word. I was only a minute or two into my monologue when I found myself unable to do anything but gag and splutter; while trying to deal with some considerable pain I had suddenly developed in my throat. I clutched my throat and swayed dramatically and mouthed words for all I was worth. I was very scared and very much in pain: but no doubt looking for all the world as if I was one of those mediums that embodied the title 'Drama Queen'. I was convinced that my group thought I was faking something, but I was *not*. I want to say that I felt as if my throat had been cut; but never having had my throat cut, I can only say that I felt as if I felt as if my throat had been cut. I hope you follow.

I had to leave the séance. I was extremely rattled by the whole episode: not only by the pain and the inability to speak coherently, but also by the brooding presence of de Soulis, who had said some things to me that I couldn't possibly repeat in polite company, and won't do so here, either. Suffice it to say that they were mostly of four letters and included suggestions about what he thought I should do and how he thought I should do it. Anatomically they were impossible and morally they were reprehensible. I went outside to get some fresh air, considerably shaken and scared. Later, when I felt well enough to rejoin everyone, I met up with the other mediums. They had all been in different parts of the building and out of earshot when I'd had my encounter with de Soulis.

When I told my story to the mediums, *Amanda* went white. *Amanda* had been working as the lead medium with another group and had been operating in a room well away from my group. There was not a chance she could have heard what was happening to me, even if she'd had her ear to the (several feet thick) walls of our room. Now *Amanda* has morals that would-be Saints might aspire to, and I have never known her to tell even a little white lie, let alone a great big fib. 'Impeccable character' is a good way to sum her up. I knew that she had not had any knowledge of my séance until I told her.

Amanda's group was also looking considerably paler after I had told them my story. When *Amanda* told me what had happened in her séance, I felt the color drain from my face again. She had picked up the presence of an unpleasant and frightening Spirit, who had hogged her séance. He had intimated that he already knew some of the investigation team and then went on to reveal that his dearest wish was to corner one of us and slit their throat. As you can see, subtlety was not his forte. As far as a spirit can achieve something as physical as a throat-slitting, de Soulis had done his very best, and it was me he had done it to. After *Amanda's* story I had no doubt of that.

I was absolutely amazed, if the truth be told. Until the point where *Amanda* told me what had happened in her séance, I thought that perhaps the atmosphere was getting to me and I needed a long lie down with a glass of something reviving (preferably alcoholic). I thought I was losing the plot, as one tends to do if one is reasonably sane and then feels that a dead person is cutting their throat. Needless to say, after speaking to *Amanda*, I revised my opinion. I left the dungeon as soon as I politely could, hoping never to go back. Talking with Spirits is one thing, but being their victim in a ghostly attempted murder is quite another.

Witness Statement 1
'York Ghost Festival's second year coincided with 400th anniversary of the Gunpowder Plot, and so, in the home city of Guye Fawkes, it seemed appropriate to theme it around him. This involved extending the festival to cover November 5, and choosing venues in places

connected to him.

'Our first choice was the Ebor Inn *at Bishopthorpe as he'd lived in this village on the outskirts of York for a short while. The second night we went to* Ye Olde Starre Inn *in the heart of York, the back beer garden would have been within yards, if not on the spot, of the location of his place of birth. Finally, the grand finale on November 5 was to be at York Dungeon. We chose the Dungeon as it was a bigger venue for our charity event, and it has a dedicated Guye Fawkes room containing tableaux of key scenes from his ultimate demise.*

'Like Diana, I had attended séance nights there regularly in the past, and so had a good idea of what we could be letting ourselves in for. Dru and James had also been there, but everybody else was going in to investigate for the first time, and this included one medium at her first ever investigation!

'The night had been quite eventful up until the final part, which was two séances being run in separate areas of the building. The layout of this horror waxworks allowed us to work either as one large group or split down. Although we'd tried working in small, separate groups before we'd never had two groups this size (fourteen in each group) running in the same building. If you believe in the energies of the group increasing the chances of paranormal activity, then this would mean an increased chance of something happening.

'Diana led the group based in the Torture Room (!), just outside the Guye Fawkes room. I took a group (with Amanda, *James,* Dru *and* Angi) *through a set of thick double doors, round a corner, up a staircase, and through the rooms along the next corridor looking for somewhere with enough space for us. What I'm trying to explain is that we weren't close enough to hear each other, and this was before we carried two way radios with us as standard. We ended up in the ante-chamber of the Plague Doctor's room, which put us not only on different levels, but with five or six walls, a staircase and several empty rooms between us.*

'We had chosen a room with enough space for us to sit down on the

stone floor; not the most ideal circumstances for a séance but we at least thought we'd give it a go. There was a strange feeling of preternatural cold, but then we're sat on stone and it's the early hours of the morning, our body energy is running low and so we're going to feel the cold more. Amanda was my lead medium for this séance, and after a quiet start she started to feel very uncomfortable. At first she seemed reluctant to share what was happening with us – and for good reason.

'She was aware of the strength of the spirit and his malevolence, and was trying to hold him back. He was looking for a way in, showing her images of what he wanted to do to one of us, and she didn't want to frighten the members of the public with us by revealing the exact details. We debated stopping so as not to allow this creature through, as Dru, James and I thought it would be one of the two evil spirits we had encountered here before, but we didn't know which one and it was getting increasingly more difficult to talk about it without revealing our worries. It was as we stopped and broke the circle that we heard footsteps coming our way. I walked out to meet them – mainly because some people weren't sure if they were real or ghostly. I took a chance on them being real – and I was right.

'The footsteps were made by two people from the other group, asking us to come back, as Diana wasn't feeling very well. Once we were sure she was not in need of any medical help, and she'd had chance to regain her voice, we told the reunited groups the stories from previous séances there and who we thought it was most likely to be: 'Bad Lord de Soulis.'

'Amanda's vision had included de Soules/Soulis (he is known under both spellings) slitting somebody's throat: a woman's throat. She had told me this before the two groups rejoined (and therefore before she knew about Diana's experience). From our perspective, we had Amanda's description of events in the séance, the testimonies of Diana's group and a photograph somebody had taken of Diana looking like she had been physically attacked – due to the swelling that had appeared on her face. Whilst you can doubt one *person's account of a spirit's behavior at an investigation, it's harder to deny it in the face of the evidence we saw that night.*

'We have, since that night, tried running duel séances again; but we've never had the same connection between the two.'

Rachel Lacy – paranormal investigator and York's Ghost Finder General.

Witness Statement 2

'I was working as a medium in York Dungeon during York Ghost Festival. The event allowed the general public to be part of a genuine ghost hunt - and séances are very much a part of the experience. On the night in question, I had conducted a séance with my group in a separate part of the building to the other groups. It had been eventful, to say the least. I had tuned in to a seemingly malevolent male spirit that was eagerly expressing the desire to harm one of us. He was quite graphic in his communication - apparently he favoured a throat-cutting and was hoping to get the opportunity!

'After this rather disturbing session, I rejoined the other groups. It was then that I learnt of the events in Diana's group. I could not believe what I was hearing!

'Whilst I was picking up the murderous spirit in my group, Diana was simultaneously going through the experience of having her throat cut. The events were synchronized, although neither of us knew this until afterwards. This may seem incredible, but it all seemed very real to me and Diana was visibly shaken by the experience. There is no way that she could possibly have heard what was happening in my group and she was as white as a sheet when I met up with her. I found the coincidence staggering and I am still at a loss to explain it rationally.'

Amanda **– medium and ghost investigator**

I didn't get my wish of either the long lie down or of never going back to York Dungeon, but I didn't encounter de Soulis again. I knew he had been around Rachel, but I never connected with him personally again. Maybe I didn't come across him because I didn't get to do many public séances after that. Maybe it's because he got bored and had found someone else to threaten. There are lots of maybes and, as with all ghost investigations, lots of unanswered questions. I'm just glad that Bad Lord de Soulis left my life for good. At least, I hope he did...

'The consequence of our crimes long survive their commission, and, like the ghosts of the murdered, forever haunt the steps of the malefactor'
Sir Walter Scott, Scottish novelist, poet and historian, 1771–1832

The Man in Black

Angela is the most frustrating, but the bubbliest of characters. A pretty, svelte blonde with a tiny frame, she has the gift of the gab and once you've spoken to her, you'll never forget her. She is always late for everything, always opinionated, but always, always, great fun and serious about ghost investigation. Her seriousness regarding ghost investigation is a quality that comes in most useful, as she is a medium. At the time of this particular event, Angela was having some supernatural disturbance at her own home and she had invited a team of us over to see what they could pick up.

In my opinion she was very brave to do this. It is all very well picking up a plethora of paranormal phenomena in someone else's abode, but finding out what people think you have in *your* house is a little unnerving. When the flight cases are packed away and the investigation is over, you still have to sleep there. I can honestly say that I had never been that keen to stay in Angela's house. Angela is an excellent hostess so you can be assured that the reason for my reticence to sleep over was not the quality of her coffee. The main reason for my desire to stay well away from her house was the Man in Black – but I didn't know what spirit presence I was picking up at the time. I just knew that there was something very creepy within her four walls – and that I wanted nothing whatsoever to do with it.

On the night of our investigation, we had quite a team of people gathered in Angela's comfortable, slightly chintzy living room. Angela could usually round up a crowd easily; she was very hard to turn down. We also had the mandatory flight cases and a night shot camcorder rigged on the stairway. The camcorder had been set up and locked off (fixed in one position) so that anyone not working upstairs could see what was happening there. They could also be assured that any movement on the screen was not camera jiggle. If we got bored, we could also participate in 'orb spotting' on the camcorder – a favorite pastime of ghost investigators. It's like watching paint dry, but with spots. The main part of the investigation was being conducted on the first floor of the cottage, as that was where Angela had insisted the problems were occurring. It was also where we had located the most anomalies on our equipment.

Several of the team had gone upstairs to see what they could see and what they could pick up. I'd avoided joining them up to this point because I am, by nature, a scaredy-cat. I need considerable cajoling before I will face anything that might be scary. I could sense there was something not very nice in the upper front of the house, and I wanted to avoid going there at all costs. However, I was not permitted to avoid it for long. The team kept on at me until I was finally convinced I should venture up to 'the area' where activity had been witnessed.

Let me explain, before we go any further, about how you should treat a medium when they are attending a ghost investigation.

- **Firstly**: never, ever, tell them anything about the building or plot being investigated. It may help them to get hit after hit, but it does nothing to verify their ability and nothing to convince anyone of the existence of life after death.

- **Secondly**: never, ever, tell them anything you have seen yourself if you can avoid it. This is for all the same reasons.

- **Thirdly**: if they are called Diana, give them a break, they are probably scared witless!

Follow these rules and you may well find that an honest medium is a useful addition to an investigation team.

With some trepidation, I made my way up to the landing. You don't have to work as a psychic to be able to feel an atmosphere – we all do it all of the time, but not usually in the sort of conditions a ghost hunter may find themselves in. The atmosphere on the stairs was creepy. I think it would be easy for anybody to hurriedly find reasons not to go up them, no matter how skeptical they are. The house is charming, but the stairs are just odd – you can't help but feel as if someone is watching you. When I finally got to the landing (I hadn't hurried!), I could immediately feel that the atmosphere had changed from the one I had been enjoying below. The pleasant, warm and sociable ambience of the lounge was long forgotten and replaced by a colder, denser, thicker feel to the air. I felt very lonely, but paradoxically, felt as if I was not alone. I shouted to the guys downstairs that I was in position and they confirmed they could see me on the TV screen. I started to 'tune in'.

At this point I'll explain what I mean by tuning in, in case you're not sure what this popular term means. If you are interested in the paranormal and the work of mediums and psychics, you will have heard the phrase before. Even so, you may not know what is going on when a medium does this. It simply means that the person is using their own method to relax and allow their mind to clear of day-to-day thoughts. It is a way of slowing down the incessant dialogue of the mind. Quietening the mind is essential if you want to make contact with discarnate spirits, so every medium will know how to do this, and many will have trained for years in order to be able to do so.

The method whereby a medium or psychic achieves a relaxed state will vary, and vary as much as the way the medium dispenses information once he or she has received it. I am clairsentient, which means that I pick up feelings and atmospheres. When I say that I 'see' a Spirit, I am not actually seeing them at all, but the feelings that I am connecting to tell me what they look like. Trying to explain any further would be as fruitless as trying to understand how someone who has been blind from birth can see blue – but at least you may have a vague idea.

When I tune in, I concentrate on my mind's eye. This is the place where you see images that are created when you hear, recite or read words. If you want to find your mind's eye, just start to describe how you get to your nearest shop from where you are now. As you describe the route, you will automatically see pictures which prompt your memory. These pictures form in your mind's eye.

When I concentrate on this spot, I imagine a clear screen, or a white fog. I allow images to form, constantly telling myself that I want to connect to any spirits that are present in the building I am investigating. Images or feelings will then come forward, although it is normally feelings, despite the fact that I am concentrating on the spot where images form. In your case, you may be lucky and see images. In some cases you will see spirits with your eyes too, but this is rare. Tuning in, for me, is stilling my mind of extraneous thoughts, concentrating on the task in hand and focusing on my mind's eye. Other mediums may tell you different, but that doesn't mean their method is any less valid.

So, having tuned in to the area upstairs in Angela's house, I could instantly pick up a male spirit. He was wearing a tall top hat, a black frock coat and he scared me stupid. I felt a brooding malevolence, but combined with an impotence to act that made him even scarier. His presence was, in the main, concentrated on the master bedroom, so I could see why Angela had felt uncomfortable in her house. I tried to push his energies away from me and pick up on something else, which seemed to work for a while. The Man in Black was strong and insistent, but I persevered and managed to get him out of my head and my space. At least temporarily...

Authentic Orbs

'How often have I said to you that when you have eliminated the impossible, whatever remains, however improbably, must be the truth?'
Sir Arthur Conan Doyle (Sherlock Holmes: *The Sign of Four*, 1890)

My work on the landing ended up being worthwhile for our investigation after all, as I had an extraordinary experience, one which certainly made me think that some credence should be given to the phenomenon of orbs. 'Orbs' are spherical objects that appear on visual recording media when they have not been seen at the time the image was recorded. You can find them often on digital cameras, but they also appear on camcorder tape, SLR camera and even disposable cameras. In my opinion, 90% of orbs are nothing more than dust, pollen, moisture or insects. I get so many pictures of orbs sent to me to assess that to say I'm bored sick of them doesn't express the depth of my feeling about them. Most of them can be dismissed. A few are more interesting, but as I don't have the equipment to assess them properly (or the scientific know-how) I still can't say they are 'paranormal', but I can *occasionally* get a kick out of the fact that I am seeing something I really do suspect may be paranormal in origin. At Angela's house I saw the first orb that I believed was the real deal.

After dismissing the Man in Black, I picked up the spirit of a woman. She was frustrated and distraught and was desperately looking for something. I allowed the lady to 'come close to me' (share my space, a bit like the movie *Ghost*, but without me having to vacate my body myself, or behave like Whoopi Goldberg). She told me she was looking for a ring with an intaglio (a semi-precious stone with an engraved picture or inscription) and that she wanted me to help her find it, it was so important to her. I wandered around some of the rooms with her. Not surprisingly to me, she didn't go in the master bedroom. After a while I realized that the search was fruitless and that she had repeated it many, many times; but I also discovered that I was becoming as desperate as her to find the ring. I was letting her come just a bit too close to me. I shouted to my colleagues that I was cutting contact with her (they were still filming everything) and did so immediately, grateful to be rid of the longing to try to achieve something that was obviously impossible. Then I went downstairs.

When I got downstairs, my colleagues were sitting staring at the video screen with blank, disbelieving looks on their faces. When they played back the video I found out why. I could see myself clearly and could hear audio playing back my commentary on my experiences. I could see and hear the point where I said that I was cutting contact with the woman, and it was at this point that I was gripped by what happened to the picture on the screen. At the very moment I had dismissed the spirit of the woman, an orb appeared clearly on the recording: exiting my solar plexus area. It didn't fly round it, nor hover over it...it moved through it and out of it. What was more extraordinary was that it did so at exactly the same time that I said I was cutting contact, you could hear my voice saying so on the video! The orb was coming out of my body: you could see each stage of the orb getting bigger. How can an object do that – pass through solid matter? I am not a scientist, but the video dumbfounded me and the fact that the incident happened at exactly the moment I released the spirit of the woman was nothing short of amazing, in my opinion. Hence, I do believe that orbs can be the Spirits of the dead, but I think that their appearance is a lot less common that the internet or television would have you believe. Now we'll return to the Man in Black. I did not hear any more from him that night and because his presence seemed to have disappeared, I thought that I could dismiss him and forget him. A few weeks later I found out that he may have been forgotten but he was not gone...

Murderous Intentions

'Often an entire city has suffered because of an evil man.'
Hesiod – Greek oral poet and economist, 800BC

'A few weeks later', after I had picked up the spirit of the Man in Black, a team of us decided to take a trip to London, England, to see what we could find at some haunted venues. It is always preferable to be able to investigate a building overnight because you are less likely to be disturbed and there is a much better atmosphere. If we couldn't work during the night, we'd still investigate if we could. We went to our chosen locations as tourists, with the addition of a few pieces of equipment. The plan was to visit the Tower of London and perhaps a few other places along the way.

Some of our team on the London trip will now be familiar to you. *Marcus* was holding court, along with Angela and I. We also had some members of our ghost club along, including Heather, who was very enthusiastic and had a great sense of humor. We made the long trip up to London by car (guess who was driving) and had a thoroughly enjoyable visit to the Tower of London, where we managed to capture some orbs and also (allegedly) picked up the spirit of Sir Walter Raleigh. A bonus to our trip was the sighting of a handsome man in uniform on the tower walls. Another bonus was that he was living, but sadly nothing more came of this encounter – I was especially disappointed.

After our visit to the Tower (I was to return at another date, and have a much more fruitful, controlled, private and after-hours investigation), we decided to go up to the Whitechapel / Spitalfields area of London. Angela had felt drawn to the 'Jack the Ripper' case and thought we might pick up something there. We found *The Ten Bells* pub, and, as it served the purpose of being the perfect location for a lunchtime drink as well as allowing us the opportunity to indulge in a surreptitious investigation, we took some seats there. We duly fought our way to the bar for our beverages, admiring the Victorian tiling on the walls and taking in the unique East London atmosphere.

History of the Ten Bells Public House

A public house has stood on the site since 1752, but was rebuilt during the 1800s. Much of the interior has been removed, but the pub is still resplendent with tiling so favored during that time. Its name is derived from the competition between Christ Church, Spitalfields and St Bride's Church, Fleet Street. Both claim to have the finest peal of bells. Christ Church was built in 1714, when it had only one bell. These were added to over the years and the pub's name is in commemoration of the addition of the tenth bell. The church only has eight bells now.

Between 1976 and 1988, the public house was named *The Jack the Ripper* and some memorabilia relating to the case was on display there. However, a long campaign was launched to get the name changed back and finally the brewery conceded and it reverted. It was known as a haunt of two Jack the Ripper victims: Annie Chapman and Mary Kelly.

As we were sitting and chatting, I started to feel very, very odd. I had been down to the toilets to see what I could sense (spiritually!) and had felt the faint spirit of a 'lady of the night', but little else. Now, suddenly, I was feeling something much more intense, and much more threatening. I should add, at this point, that my drink consisted of lemonade. I had not ingested anything that would impair my ability to understand the real from the unreal, or impair my ability to drive us all home safely and legally.

As we were in the pub to investigate, I allowed the spirit that I was sensing to come a little closer to me – discovering too late that this was a grave error. Although my spirit guide at the time did not take any funny business when it came to spirits and my protection, it seems she was simply pushed out of the way by a determined, dark and somewhat dangerous entity that had decided to home in on me.

I found myself mesmerized and quite 'out of it' when this spirit approached me, and my own spirit shrank back in fear as 'he' slowly took me over. Of course, this probably sounds like dramatic prose and nothing else – in fact it *is* dramatic prose; but it is also the truth. I could sense the brooding figure; he had dark eyes and grayish hair, a black top hat and a fairly long thin nose. Although I could see him, I really felt as if he was sharing space with my own 'soul', that he was 'in' me and looking out. It seems that my feelings were not without basis. As I turned to look at my friends and ask if they could help me understand what was going on, I was surprised to see that Angela and Heather were staring at me. It appears that they could see this man that had invaded my space with their own eyes.

This will sound completely crazy to you if you are a novice to the work of mediums, but it is actually a fairly common phenomenon. Known as transfiguration, the usual technique is for the medium to fall into a trance and allow the spirits to take him or her over, the result being the appearance of the spirit's features over that of the medium. Many mediums seem to be able to do this at will, but will normally conduct their transfiguration sessions in a dimly-lit room, and usually with special lighting. For me, the transfiguration was happening spontaneously, in a well-lit room – and there are still occasions when it happens spontaneously to me today. You'll read of some more occurrences of this phenomenon later.

Heather and Angela seemed transfixed, particularly Angela

who was staring at me. It was then that one of the most peculiar conversations I'd ever heard commenced, between Angela and I (the 'I' being the male spirit that was sharing my space).

It became obvious that this spirit was very drawn to Angela and wanted to monopolize her. Interspersed between snippets of his history (he'd spent some time in the US, but he lived in London; he was a 'gentleman') he tried his best to control Angela and dominate her. Angela wasn't having any of it. She said that she could see my eyes were not mine, realized I was not acting and told the man exactly where he could go and how he could get there. He was not put off. He gave her the impression that he already knew her – and it was then that the truth of the matter dawned. He had been the Man in Black that had been haunting her cottage, although now it appeared that it was not the cottage he was attracted to, but her! I was just his convenient hostess and I was *not* honored to have his attentions. At least I knew he was haunting me to get to Angela, but knowing the reason did not make me more comfortable.

He stayed with me for around an hour, during which time I had the peculiar sensation of feeling at least a foot taller than I was in reality. I also felt incredibly powerful and morals didn't seem that important. It became obvious that the man with me was both clever and dangerous. He had dropped pretty heavy hints that murder was not something that bothered him. In fact, he implied he'd had a few attempts at it while he was living, with some fairly spectacular results. As the conversation progressed, we realized the significance of the encounter - that is, why he had come to me while we were in *The Ten Bells*. It was not a place that was unfamiliar to him; in fact it was somewhere he had visited often when he was still living. He had a fascination with the Jack the Ripper murders, and suggested that he was in fact the Ripper himself!

By this time, the whole group was taken aback and somewhat worried, it seems that all of us could see or sense the spirit and many of us were joining in the confrontation with him. The regular punters at the pub must have thought we were barking mad, and looking over what I've written about the encounter, I can see why!

'Jack the Ripper'
Jack the Ripper is the pseudonym given to one of the most famous serial killers in history. The murders attributed to 'Jack' occurred in the Whitechapel area of London, UK, in 1888 and were typically committed on female prostitutes. The throats of the victims were cut and then the body was mutilated; sometimes the internal organs were removed. The Jack the Ripper cases were never solved and over a hundred theories about the identity of the murderer exist today.

Five murders are ascribed to 'Jack' - although other later murders have also been suggested.

Mary Ann Nichols
Mary's body was found on August 31, 1988. Her throat had been cut twice and the lower part of her body had been ripped open.

Annie Chapman
Annie's body was found on September 8, 1888 in a doorway. Her throat had also been slit twice and her torso was slashed open. Her uterus had been removed.

Elizabeth Stride
Elizabeth's body was found on September 30 1888. The main artery on the left side of her neck had been severed.

Catherine Eddowes
Catherine's body was also found on September 30, about three-quarters of an hour after Elizabeth's. Her throat had been cut and her torso ripped open. One kidney and most of her uterus had

been removed.

Mary Jane Kelly

Mary was found on November 9 1888. Her throat had been cut down to the spine and her abdomen had been emptied of most of its organs. Her heart had also been removed.

It must seem a bit daft to you to hear me recall how I felt the spirit of a man who claimed to be Jack the Ripper inside me. Dafter still, maybe, to hear that there was a full-on conversation progressing with this man and my colleagues. Doubtless you are wondering why no-one had called the ambulance service without delay: to investigate the possibilities of a straight-jacket for me. I'm sorry, but my excuse is the same in this chapter as it is in others: you had to be there. This man was very real, was giving out information that could turn out to be of use in the 21st Century, and he was stalking Angela and I and we wanted him to desist, forthwith.

So, did we get rid of the Man in Black? Even more importantly, did he reveal who he was? Most importantly – was he the Ripper? 'Yes' is the answer to the former two questions, and, in my opinion, 'no' to the latter.

After some effort, we did persuade the man's spirit to leave. With a combination of my guide's help, my own efforts, my friends' determination and our departure from *The Ten Bells* we managed to rid ourselves of his presence.

We also managed to determine who the spirit was. His image was clear enough to me for me to be able to find a picture of him and the snippets of history he revealed matched that of the man I had found. In fact, the image of James Maybrick was an incredible likeness of the Man in Black. My colleagues also confirmed his appearance. James Maybrick was one of the suspects in the Jack the Ripper case.

So do I think that James Maybrick was the Ripper? No. In my opinion he liked the idea of notoriety and power, but I do not think he was. I think he had issues with women and his own virility (or lack of it), but I do not think he committed any murders. I do think he was a dangerous man, though, and I think he could perhaps have become quite deranged if he had lived any longer. But I don't think he murdered those girls in Victorian London – and I'm afraid I don't know who did. I had one more visit from Maybrick before he disappeared from my life – hopefully forever.

A month or so after our London trip, I was working in my shop (I had a shop for Pagans, in York, England), when I was suddenly 'taken over' by the strong spirit of a man, a man I recognized only too well. It was the Man in Black, James Maybrick, who assured me he would continue to contact me and that he had more to tell me. It scared me so much I persuaded a friend to accompany me home and stay with me until I had fallen asleep, but I didn't hear from Maybrick again. I am not sorry about that. To date I have not heard of him contacting anyone who had been with me on the other occasions he'd come through; so maybe he's finished what he wanted to accomplish, or maybe our guides (and us) are just getting smarter. As long as he stays away, I don't care why.

History of James Maybrick

James Maybrick was a well-to-do gentleman who resided in Liverpool, and was involved in the cotton industry. He was one of six brothers, of whom only four survived into adulthood. James married Florence (Florie) Chandler after meeting her on a voyage from New York to Liverpool. She was the daughter of a rich family, and was used to the very best things in life. James was expected to continue to provide these, and it seems that trying to do so was a constant strain on him. He was an abuser of arsenic and strychnine (both fashionable in Victorian England as cure-alls and increasers of virility), with arsenic being particularly dangerous and also addictive.

Florie and James had two children: a boy called James and a girl called Gladys Evelyn. There was potential for a happy family life, but things were not going so well with James' finances and he and Florie had numerous disagreements; some of them provoking violence in James. He had been recorded as giving her a black eye on at least one occasion.

James also kept a mistress for a good part of their marriage, although records suggest it is possible that his mistress was, in fact, his first wife and that there could be some bigamy at work. Eventually Florie took a lover too, but was less cautious about the details of her affair and was found out. To cut a long story short, Florie was accused of murdering James by poisoning and sentenced to hang. It appears that, although she was convicted; the trial was a travesty and she was released.

James Maybrick was not a suspect in the Ripper case until a 'diary' claiming to be by him was found in 1992. The authenticity of this diary is still debated, but it is considered by most to be a hoax. It does show consistency with the facts of the trial and, if he really did write it, shows a lot of the character he showed to my colleagues and I on the few occasions we had the 'pleasure' of his company. Why he was sensed in Lancashire (the cottage), London (*The Ten Bells*) and York (my shop) I'm not sure. I thought that I was simply a go-between so that he could get to Angela, but Angela was not present in my shop on his final visit.

Dealing with the Discarnate

*'The evil of the world is made possible by nothing but the sanction
you give it.'*
Ayn Rand, author, *Atlas Shrugged*

So, if you are unfortunate enough to make contact with a spirit
or entity that is negative (or with my luck, downright
malevolent!), how do you deal with it?

Firstly, let me make it clear that contact with these types of
spirits is extremely rare. The reason we hear so many stories
about them is a bit like why the news is always full of tragedy.
Humankind seems more interested in stories of things that go
wrong, than in stories of hope and happiness. If you think I'm
wrong, mull this over while you are at the back of a huge traffic
jam caused by people slowing down to see who has been
mangled at the scene of an accident. Horror and evil seems to be
a popular form of entertainment, so it is no surprise that contact
with negative energies makes news, and contact with spirits that
can inform and uplift us doesn't. We only hear the negative
stories; hence they appear a lot more common than they are.

Secondly, you have to bear in mind that I have attended
literally hundreds of ghost investigations and have gone out of
my way to be at places that are known to be haunted by powerful
entities. It's a numbers game; if you attend enough ghost hunts,
something will happen eventually.

Thirdly, let me remind you of an old adage that you have
probably heard, but perhaps not really paid any attention to:

'The dead can't hurt you; it is the living you should be afraid of!' This is so true, the chances of any spirit having the energy, ability, or real desire to try to harm a living person is so slim that the chances of it happening to you are almost zero. The living, however, are much more likely to be able to hurt you, so if you really feel you need to be afraid of something, be afraid of them!

So, assuming you do come across a being from the other worlds that seems out to try to do you some harm – what do you do? Well, the technique I'll give you for shutting out these entities will also protect you whenever you go ghost hunting; and is worth using regardless of what you believe you may encounter. It will harm no-one and no-thing, but will make sure that you are spiritually and psychically safe. You don't need to be religious to use this technique, but belief in a deity or deities will certainly add to the protection that you are surrounding yourself with. You can set up this psychic shield before you go to the ghost hunt and you can also enhance your protection during the ghost hunt by repeating the procedure.

The Psychic Shield Technique

1. Sit quietly if you can, trying to relax by concentrating on each part of your body – in your mind. Focus on your toes, calves, thighs, etc., and tell yourself that the part you are concentrating on is relaxing entirely. Feel the stress and tension flowing out from it and down into the ground. Know that you are relaxing enough to be able to reach the psychic and spiritual part of yourself.

2. When you feel you are fully relaxed, imagine, in your mind's eye, a pillar of light flowing into the very top of your head from the sky above. See it shining, pulsing and flowing. You may find that it is white, silver or gold; any of these colors are protective and a symbol of higher energies and powers.

72

3. In your mind's eye, see this color touch the top of your head and watch the light flow down all around you, right down to your toes and underneath them through the ground, creating a glowing force field of protective power. See yourself cocooned in an egg of brilliant light.

4. Now see that egg shape grow in intensity and size, so that you can feel the protective power.

5. At this point, if you have a deity or deities, ask Him / Her / Them to help you to protect yourself from any negative entities. You may say a prayer for yourself and for all others attending if you wish.

6. Remind yourself, preferably out loud, that you are now fully protected and that the shield will protect you and dispel negative entities. Then allow yourself to gently return to everyday consciousness.

7. During the ghost hunt (and especially during any séance or Ouija board), make sure that you visualize your shield and imagine it glowing brighter and expanding.

A few further tips:

• Don't court or 'play' with any negative energy that you encounter. Deny them and back off. The power of your righteous anger or your curiosity will just feed them and allow them to play mind games with you. Ignore them and walk away, enhancing your psychic shield as you go;

• Remember that you have angelic and spiritual protection to call upon. Ask for help from the angels and your spirit guides – they can help you, but only if you ask;

- If you are really feeling frightened, repeat out loud Psalm 121. You do not have to be Christian to do this. This powerful charm will call in protection for you regardless of your religious persuasions. It is important that you put as much belief in divine support as possible while you do this. If you get this right, you may feel an energy-form manifest behind you: this is angelic protection coming to your aid and is there to help you.

Another thing to remember is that the majority of the negative entities that you may come across were human. That means that they will behave in the same manner as a bully might in the living world. Bullies rely on fear more than anything else, closely followed by a desire to be heard. They are most definitely attention-seeking.

Make sure that you take away those things they desire most. Don't show them fear and don't allow them to become the center of attention. The more energy you put into trying to reason with them or even acknowledging their presence, the more you are likely to give them a reason to continue with their anti-social behavior.

If you're really uncomfortable and you have tried all the methods above – leave the place. I know this may seem an obvious thing to do, but some people seem to be under the impression that they just can't go until they have dealt with whatever type of entity they've come across. Yes, you can! I've done it often enough myself and I've lived to tell the tale. This may seem like my cowardice working overtime, but that is only true to a degree. There are some cases where it is best to leave and get in the professionals. These cases are rare; the chances of you being persecuted by a ghost that is so malevolent you need a rescue medium or an exorcist is highly unlikely. However, I have briefly covered both areas for your interest.

Rescue and Exorcism

If you have trouble with a particularly nasty and possibly even dangerous ghost – 'who ya gonna call?' Well yes, there are some groups who claim to be 'Ghostbusters', but in the main you would need to look for either a rescue medium or an exorcist. The decision on who to call on is not necessarily a matter of faith, even though it may seem to be. Certainly, the majority of exorcists will be Christian Clergy, as the rite of exorcism is very much their thing. Rescue Mediums are often Spiritualists, but this is not always the case. A faith is usually required for either method, but it is not a prerequisite that the person calling out the rescue medium or exorcist has a faith themselves, although it does help.

Rescue

This term refers to what happens when a medium's attempt to move a spirit to 'where they should be' is successful. The medium connects with the troublesome spirit and will usually attempt to find out what is troubling them and why they will not move on from haunting to a 'higher plane'. When this information has been gleaned, the spirit has usually said their piece and will be in a more co-operative state of mind. The medium will then try to move them on to where they should have gone when they died (Heaven or its equivalent).

Of course, it takes a good bit of belief to accept the premise of rescue in the first place and as you are unlikely to have any immediate proof that a rescue has been successful, you will need faith that things will get better, too. For someone who calls out a rescue medium, the only proof possible is if the phenomena experienced ceases entirely.

Most rescue mediums acknowledge the existence of an afterlife in another plane or dimension. The spirits that they come into contact with have not reached this place and are still connected to our world, for whatever reason. Theories about why some human spirits do not naturally pass onto another realm of existence vary. They include:

- An attachment to a person or building;

- A traumatic death;

- A quick death, resulting in them being unaware they have died;

- Something left unfinished from their earthly life, or guilt.

Some of these theories seem supported by messages received from rescue mediums – but of course the whole thing is very subjective and there is no proof of the existence of ghosts, let alone why they are here.

I think it is fairly common knowledge that the vast majority of people who claim to have had a near-death experience have reported seeing a great light, often emanating peaceful and loving energies. When the rescue medium attempts to persuade the spirit to move on, they look for a light.

At this point you may wonder why a rescue medium would look for a 'light' if the spirit appears to be of a malevolent disposition. Surely the light comes from Heaven? No evil person will be going there, will they?

From my own experience, the light is offered to all spirits, regardless of their behavior here on earth. I have never encountered any evidence of a hell waiting for the departed – no matter how evil they appear to be. My own conclusions are that if there is a hell, it is created by us. Evil spirits will create their own hell and will be faced with their deeds in a very personal way; sometimes reliving them. Once they have experienced enough of this to realize the ramifications of their behavior on others they will have the option to pass on to the light in the same way as every other spirit.

So rescue involves a medium acting as a mediator and helping the spirit to pass to the life it should have on the 'other side'. The spirit is not punished, is not exiled – it is simply helped to move on.

Exorcism

Exorcism is an extreme method for removing negative entities. It does not help them to pass on to the afterlife; it banishes them from this realm. Where they actually end up depends on what you personally believe. Usually exorcism is a ritual, which is undertaken by a member of the clergy. It is mostly Christians that perform the rite, although Buddhists and Hindus have their own versions. The practitioners of exorcism are usually of the belief that the spirit is really some kind of demon or devil and are therefore quite happy to banish it with no thought of where it might go – as long as it is sent away from earth. This is fine if the spirit is a demon or devil (assuming there are such things); but if they were once human and very misguided, then a rescue might be a better option. You must formulate your own opinion.

As I am not a member of the Christian Clergy, I am not privy to the ritual used in exorcism and I do not claim to be an authority on the subject at all. I believe the ritual involves invoking the name of Jesus and of God and some versions ask for support from the Angels – in particular the Archangel Michael – but my knowledge is sketchy, to say the least. If you want to know more, then I suggest you speak to the experts: the exorcists themselves.

Usually exorcism is employed to deal with possession; but it can be used to rid a place of a negative entity that exists within the four walls, rather than within the owner.

If you have exhausted all possibilities of attempting to persuade an entity to leave you alone (sometimes just asking works wonders!) then you might be inclined to want to call an exorcist. You can usually find an exorcist by contacting your local clergy. Anglican clergy as well as Catholic often offer this service. You may be able to find a rescue medium by looking on the internet. I am not aware of any fees being levied by the clergy and most rescue mediums will only ask for travel expenses, which is fair enough. I would suggest you attempt to check out credentials for a rescue medium before you request their help; but this is notoriously difficult as there are no formal qualifications for someone who works in this field. Use your common sense: if you can possibly get references, get them!

Chapter 6
Past Lives Remembered

If you have read the title of this book and the subsequent chapter 'What is a ghost?' then you may be wondering exactly what Past Lives have to do with ghost hunting. You'd be right to wonder – very often they have nothing whatsoever to do with it. However, in two of the experiences I am going to present to you, spirits were involved, and the other experience was just so shocking, I felt I couldn't leave it out.

It is very difficult, whether you are a skeptic or a believer, to take part in a ghost hunt and not come across other spiritual disciplines. The paranormal touches on the spiritual as it is bound to do; and you will find yourself considering all sorts of questions as you go about your ghost hunting tasks.

One of the questions you are bound to ask yourself, whether you are skeptical or not, is whether you are psychic yourself. At some point, if you attend enough investigations, you will feel something that is unlike anything you have felt before. After you have dismissed the usual suspects – tiredness, atmosphere, and hallucination – you will almost certainly come across a point where you are left still wondering what has actually happened.

The events I've recalled in this book are those which have left me wondering - after I've discounted the obvious. Attempting to rationalize them involves looking at what happened and trying to recall it without embellishment. As you can see, it is often not possible to do this easily. Past Lives are, without doubt, an area of belief that is sometimes hard to swallow. You will find it easy to locate books on the subject and they will certainly fascinate, even if they don't convince you. The best way to find out what is really true for you is always the same – experience as much as you can and formulate your own ideas.

My Wife and I

'I think reincarnation is possible. Hopefully we all get recycled.'
Christina Ricci, actress

It had been a long drive and I was late. I hate being late, and I avoid it at all costs. 'Late' brings me out in blotches, makes me hyperventilate and raises my blood pressure so that I become very, very stressed and really, really grumpy.

I guess it was my upbringing that ensured I'd never be fashionably late at parties. My parents taught me manners, and keeping someone waiting for my appearance was considered the height of rudeness. I didn't appear late for anything then, and I still can't manage 'late' today – at least not without a severe attack of nausea. I'm the person waiting an hour for a bus; not because *it's* running late, but because *I'm* running early. I'm also the person sipping a juice quietly in the kitchen at a party when you arrive. This is not because I'm shy (anyone who knows me will vouch for that!); but because I've already been there for over an hour, much to the embarrassment of the hosts who weren't even dressed when I arrived.

Unfortunately, I had been unable to avoid a delay when I set off to attend a large ghost convention. On my arrival I was already late, annoyed, hyperventilating and blotchy. I had been booked to give a very simple talk on working with pendulums plus I was listed as a reader. I would be required to give some psychic / mediumistic readings for the public as well as speak publicly. I was dreading my appearance as I knew I wasn't at my best – I don't work well when I'm cheesed off. However, despite feeling less than prepared, my talk went well and I managed to stay composed. I was also kept very busy giving readings: so busy that by the time I'd been there a few hours, I was really tired. When I eventually got to read cards for *Sally*, I was completely exhausted.

I had never seen *Sally* before in my life, nor did I know of her daughter. She was just another customer who had joined the queue to receive the few words of wisdom that I could impart. Apart from thinking 'I like you, but I've no idea why!' I just gave her a reading. The reading went very well; I had managed to successfully connect with both her current life and also with a couple of deceased relatives that meant something to her. After I had finished the reading, I decided I really needed to take a break, so I followed *Sally* out to the bar, where I ordered a coffee.

For some reason, I thought a coffee and a chat with a nice woman and her daughter would be relaxing. It did start that way. We exchanged the usual pleasantries and sipped at our drinks. The bar we were sitting in was oak paneled and very elegant, a testament to the style of a bygone age. It was full of attendees to the convention and there was a buzz of enthusiasm and light-hearted conversation making a nice accompaniment to our coffee break. I had taken a seat with my back to a grand marble fireplace, adorned with a huge vase full of flowers that had been carefully placed at the back of the very large mantelpiece. All was going very well and I had started to relax, enjoying the ambience and the welcome injection of caffeine. Suddenly, just as I'd really started to chill out, I heard a voice proclaim: 'Good God, you're my wife!'

I was so surprised to hear the voice as it seemed to be directed at *Sally*, but I couldn't see anyone near us who could have said it. Certainly, it sounded as if it came from our table, but there was only *Sally*, *Sally's* daughter and myself. I know that *Sally's* daughter didn't say it, I was pretty sure *Sally* didn't say it: so that only left me. *Sally* stared back at me. 'And you're my husband, aren't you?' she announced, quite matter-of-factly.

Finally, my brain caught up with my wayward mouth. *I* had said she was my wife and I *knew* that she was, but part of me disagreed and there was a battle going on in my head, which hurt. I found myself becoming quite detached from my personal, silent (and heated) conversation. It was just easier. I am heterosexual and at that point in my life I was a divorcee and single. Naturally, I was quite confused that my mouth was making statements that were obviously untrue and wondered if it had decided to formally separate from logic and reason or whether it was just taking a short holiday. Although you are probably thinking that I suffer from schizophrenia after reading this much of this chapter...I don't. In fact I am, to all intents and purposes, sane. The conversation in my head now spilled out and I was bemused to find that it had developed into an audible conversation with Sally.

'Do you remember when we used to come to this house?' I heard myself saying.

'Yes', said *Sally*, emphatically. 'It was so much fun!'

'And we used to ride around the grounds' (the present-day me became incredulous at the thought that 'I' had ever ridden a horse, or, more accurately, that a horse had ever allowed me to).

My mouth continued discussing this imaginary existence with *Sally*. A whole story was unfolding of Thomas and Catherine, a well-to-do young couple from the time of Charles II; who had visited the hotel we were in, when it was a hunting lodge. This couple was obviously very much in love, and very pleased to meet up again. From my standpoint (the rational, practical bit of me) it appeared that my (now out of control) mouth was one of a pair of long lost lovers. The rest of me was one of two very bemused gooseberries; who were both a little disconcerted that their insane conversation was being heard by a room full of people!

The conversation wound on, with the two parties from the 17th Century happily discussing their life, while *Sally* and I mentally looked on.

'Yes,' said Thomas (me!) 'I loved to come here and visit George. Do you remember him?'

'Yes!' said Catherine (*Sally*) 'I can ...!'

At that point Catherine's reply was drowned out by an almighty crash coming from somewhere in the vicinity of my left ear. I turned around in shock, and saw a completely destroyed flower arrangement on the floor a few inches from my chair, surrounded by shards of pottery. I was a bit shaken as it had missed me by inches and it had been a huge display, but I was still trying to come to terms with the ongoing conversation, and frankly that seemed more disturbing to me. However, the rest of the people in the bar with us seemed much more interested in the vase.

As I looked around I saw at least 30 white faces, all staring at me and at the flower display and broken vase on the floor. 'I'm fine!' I said to everyone in the room, and turned towards *Sally*. She was also looking pale.

'What's wrong with everyone?' I said, wondering why people were so amazed to see a vase fall down. 'They were nice flowers, but it wasn't our fault, the hotel will be fine with it.'

At that point one of the hotel staff dashed over. He started cleaning up the mess on his hands and knees, muttering under his breath (but loud enough for our table to hear) 'I'm never coming back to this f*****g hotel again!' He picked up the remains of the vase and flowers and dashed back behind the bar with them, continuing to complain and demonstrate a considerable knowledge of expletives. When he got back to the bar he went into another room, presumably to dispose of the broken vase and flowers. Then he came back into the bar with a few things in his hand and walked out. I didn't see him again the whole weekend and was told later that he had left that same day.

I was amazed by his behavior, and frankly, everyone else's. It was only a vase, after all, and accidents can happen. I couldn't figure out why everyone was having such a strong reaction to the destroyed flower display and why they were giving me such odd looks. Granted, the vase had only missed me by inches, but I was fine and the display could be replaced. It was *Sally* that filled me in on everyone's reaction.

'You couldn't see it, could you?' she said.

'See what?' I returned, wondering if she meant the damage to the vase.

'You couldn't see the vase levitating and being thrown at you!'

As my jaw hit the floor, she explained that as soon as I mentioned 'George', the vase behind me on the mantelpiece had lifted up a few inches and then hurled itself violently towards me. That was why everyone was staring. They'd seen the impossible behavior of the vase in an allegedly haunted hotel and reacted accordingly.

Witness Statement

'Some years ago, I attended a ghost hunter's convention in a wonderfully charismatic hunting lodge. After enjoying the festivities, a large number of us decided to have a break and enjoy the rich-smelling coffee.

'Around 30 of us were sat in the decorative lounge area, chatting away in our own small groups. Suddenly, out of the corner of my eye, I saw something move to my left. I quickly glanced to my side and was stunned (as were a number of other investigators and friends) to see a very large vase of full-bloomed flowers appear to hover briefly over the ornate mantelpiece. Then, without warning, the vase launched itself, with some force, clean across to the middle of the lounge area – a distance of some 10 feet or so.

'We were a little stunned. Some people were saying, 'Who would have thrown that?' and some like myself were saying 'WOW! Did

you see that? It flew!' I knew I had witnessed some serious paranormal activity.

'It was then it dawned on me that in a room full of investigators, not one of us had caught the event on camera as we had all been drinking coffee and on a break! The irony of this event has not been lost on me, even to this day. This is still one of the best pieces of mass-witnessed, (but not captured) phenomena that I have ever seen, to date.'

Simon Curwood - 'Most Popular Paranormal Investigator and Paranormal Medium 2009', West Wales Awards; proprietor – *Spooks Paranormal Investigators*

Shortly after the vase incident, I left the bar to return to work, but made a few enquiries about 'George' after I had finished. It appears that a certain George Villiers, Second Duke of Buckingham and confidante to Charles II, used to visit the hotel we were in when he was alive. Popular legend has it that his shade haunts there still. Even today, there are stories of what has been experienced by people who stay in certain rooms in the hotel, and they are linked with the spirit of George Villiers.

It is conceivable that George would have visited the property as he was a close friend of the king and the king had owned it. In fact, King Charles II left it as a legacy to one of his bastard children, Henry Beauclerk, First Duke of St. Albans. It is also conceivable that our 'other lives', Thomas and Catherine, would have visited the house as they were obviously gentry and known to the King.

The incident was shocking, surprising and fascinating all in one, and I couldn't leave it there. The genuine connection I felt with *Sally* hounded me long after the convention, so we kept in contact and I suggested that she came up to Yorkshire to visit me. At the same time I would arrange a past-life hypnosis session for both of us with a good friend of mine, Carole Chui. Carole is a multi-talented lady with vast experience of paranormal, magickal and spiritual subjects. She is also a qualified hypnotherapist who specializes in Past Life Regression. I called Carole when I returned home from the convention to tell her about my strange experiences and to ask her if she would be prepared to regress *Sally* and I. She, too, was fascinated by what had happened to me, and she agreed immediately.

A few weeks later, *Sally* and her family came to visit. We had a pleasant day seeing the sights and then, in the evening, travelled to the suburbs to visit Carole. After introductions and a chat, Carole took us to the room she had set aside for hypnotherapy clients, a room that was comfortable, warm and quiet. She then gave us each a couch, and talked us down into a hypnotic state.

At this point it may be worthwhile explaining what you could expect from a past-life hypnosis session.

Past Life Regression

'I intend to live forever. So far, so good.'
Steven Wright, comedian, actor and writer

Past Life Regression is a technique that investigates the theory that we have all had past lives, i.e. that we have reincarnated many times. Hypnosis is the most popular method of connecting with past lives, although guided meditations and trance are other methods that can be employed. If you decide to try Past Life Regression through hypnotherapy, ensure that you are regressed by a fully-qualified hypnotherapist, preferably one who specializes in past lives and one that is knowledgeable on the subject.

Murphy's Law
One of the best known cases of complete immersion into a past life is that of Virginia Tighe. Whilst under hypnosis, she recalled a past life as a woman named Bridget Murphy (better known as

Bridey). Her hypnotist, Morey Bernstein, released a book on the case: *The Search for Bridey Murphy*. Virginia's recall of this alleged past life was extremely detailed; she even spoke with a strong Irish accent during the regression. Although the existence of Bridey could not be completely verified (despite the huge amount of detail revealed by Virginia), this case still stands as one worth looking into. We may never know whether Bridey was an overactive imagination or a real experience, but the book and the story are extremely thought-provoking.

The Descent of Man

> 'When a man tells you that he got rich through hard work, ask him: 'Whose?''
> Don Marquis, humorist, journalist and author

Past Life Regression Hypnosis is, from my own experience, pleasurable. It brings relaxation, imparts long-forgotten knowledge and sometimes helps one to move on from traumas that have been experienced long before one came into this life. I have had several of these sessions and have always felt them to be worthwhile. I have been fascinated by the history, people, places and sights I have seen and I have learnt so much about myself as the person I am now.

I'd like to tell you about my very first past life experience, conducted in the late 1980s when I was just starting to explore the paranormal and the mystical. During this regression, I found myself as a very rich, very dandy, young country squire. Swanning about my father's estate, I looked down my angular and noble nose at most people - but in particular at ladies. Yes, dear reader, if you are not aware of the possibilities of past lives, know now that you will almost certainly experience the (dubious?) pleasure of finding yourself as a member of the opposite sex. Having a very differently shaped body is one thing, but having a totally different set of values and experience is so much more disconcerting!

My squire definitely had a different set of values and a different level of experience to my (then) 20th Century self. During our past life session the hypnotherapist leading the regression asked a number of questions, which part of me remembers answering. Because of the level of hypnosis that I naturally reach, I am aware of my past and present selves, feel the emotions of both, and experience a light level of the sounds and sights of my past self. I do not fully experience either life during regression, but share a little of both at the same time.

After I had settled into the hypnosis and was relaxed, the hypnotist asked a number of questions. One of the questions was 'Who are you with?' I told the hypnotherapist about Annie, my betrothed, who was a pretty little ball of lace and golden curls in a long, full, silken dress. The hypnotherapist asked me what I did for a living and I poured scorn on a need to do anything except be myself. Then she asked me what my companion did for a living and, to this day, I remember the tart response from my 'other' self.

'Do? **Do?** Why, she sits and sews! She doesn't **do** anything at all! She is just a woman, after all!'

My 20th Century self was appalled, outraged and furious at the words coming out of her mouth; despite the fact they were the words of another lifetime. My 18th Century self thought that the hypnotherapist was crazy to ask about a woman doing anything productive and carried on doing absolutely nothing himself. I was completely torn in my reactions to the question and answer and came out of the session with real food for thought.

In my current life, I was born into a family that was essentially a matriarchy. I didn't like matriarchy from day one. It is very sad to see grown men having to hand over their pay-packets unopened, and hoping they *may* get a little back for pocket money. That is what happened in my house. I hate sexism of any kind – whether misogyny or phylogeny (misogyny is the hatred of women and phylogeny is the hatred of men). I was vociferous about inequality then and I am now. I am as much for men's rights as women's.

Perhaps after my nobleman life ended, the Spirit of my squire realized how judgmental and wrong he had been and that's why I am how I am. Or maybe I had come into my current life to see how it feels to be on the sharp end of inequality (because I have been) and to learn the error of my former life's ways. The experience of my manly past life self struck a chord with me, whatever the reason.

The Back of Beyond

'The average man, who does not know what to do with his life, wants another one which will last forever.'
Anatole France, French poet, journalist and novelist, 1844–1924

I can still remember my regression session with *Sally* and Carole Chui. I can tell you it felt really odd to be a man in love with a young woman, but still be a woman 'watching' the scene and feeling like a gooseberry. I remember how embarrassed I was when I heard *Sally* react fully to her past life and respond to the amorous advances of my former self. I also remember the pain I felt when I discovered our relationship was (later in that life) falling apart. However, I think it best that you hear what happened from Carole herself, as she was an observer and not a player.

Witness statement
'I had been working in the area of past life exploration for some time, and it was the only reason I decided to take a hypnosis qualification. I had worked with Diana before and I eagerly agreed to take her and

Sally *through an exploration of their possible past connection. I never even gave a thought to the fact that, although I had done group regression sessions where people explained individual lifetimes when they were awoken, I had never done a regression with two people and attempted to return them both to the same past lifetime. I know that people vary in the way they react, so I was prepared for a number of reactions. Some people go very deep and speak so softly I have to hover over them to hear what they say. Others speak as though awake and even go through the full range of facial expressions. In that category I had once come across a bearded young man (in this life) who transformed into a house proud wife in ancient Rome, furious about dirt being trodden into her house!*

'However, despite my experience, I had not attempted to regress two people together, and have them speak and interact. I did not know Sally *either, so I had no idea what she would do. So, before I started the regression, I made sure* Sally *was comfortable with the process (about Diana I had no worries).* Sally *seemed self-possessed and eager to continue, so I led her and Diana through relaxation into trance, suggesting that they were going back...back into a life they had shared.*

'What happened next was extraordinary. They did indeed go back into their shared life; much to my relief. Past life regression is not like catching a train, and you cannot be sure where you will end up (or perhaps it is like catching a train!). I could not be sure that they would arrive in the same life, or if they did; that they would arrive in the same moment.

'The process worked immediately. They were ready and it was as though I was simply providing a meeting room for them outside time. In the same moment they were back, and began to act out the scene of their early meeting. For those of us in the room it was as though we were eavesdropping. Sally *became playful and flirtatious and the crackle of attraction in the room between the young man and woman (at that point we truly believed them to be a couple) was there like a presence in itself. Once I had led them into the scene,*

they played it out. There was no need for encouragement and I sat back. It was going to be easy. I just had to keep a watchful eye on how things were going.

'I moved them in time and it was sad to see love go cold and disillusion set in as their story advanced. However, when they returned to the present, there was a sense of relief. The regression had given Tom and Catherine time to interact and allowed them go back to their normal lives as Diana and Sally. There was no danger for either of them of the past becoming an obsession; and they would not find that nature had played them a cruel trick in reincarnating them both as heterosexual women. They had honored the past and moved on into their own present lives.'

Carole Chui BA D Hyp BBSCH, Clinical Hypnotherapist

After *Sally* and I had experienced our past lives, we parted on good terms and have periodically touched base to see how our current lives have progressed. I have attempted to find Thomas and Catherine and have discovered a few potential candidates, but not enough to really feel I know exactly who they are.

What I do know is that they were in love, they were very real to both *Sally* and I (don't forget, we were complete strangers the day this all started) and that without a doubt, the spirit of George Villiers knew who they were only too well...

Lean on Me

'True love is like a psychic experience. Everyone tells ghost stories, but few have ever seen a ghost'.
Anon.

For once, I was really excited about the ghost hunt we had planned for the evening. Fairly new to ghost hunting at this point in my career, I was really looking forward to the prospect of visiting a haunted house – and even better, a stately home.

The journey to the venue had been uneventful, although I had managed to get a bit lost on the way. However, the team and I still arrived at the location in good time; which is always the case if I have anything to say about our schedule! As we were early, we found a local hostelry so that we could plan the evening in advance and acquire some refreshment.

Settling back with a lemonade in my hand, I surveyed the team. Angela and *Marcus* you have already met: but on this occasion we also had Tristram, a knowledgeable and talented mystic and medium; Kerry, a local, likeable lass with a great deal of enthusiasm and common sense; and John, a stick-thin amiable guy who had just come along for the experience and was going to help us with data collection.

We also had a couple with us, who I will refer to as *'The Peabodys'*. At the time that this event took place, anyone working in the paranormal field in the North of England will have come across them at some point, whether they wanted to or not. The husband, *Fred*, was a large man with a broad Lancashire accent and an asthmatic wheeze that sounded like he was a practiced dirty phone caller. Silence can be a useful tool to use on a vigil, but if *Fred* was with you, you wouldn't get any.

Florence looked like an archetypal witch. I say this with some hesitancy, as I am a 'real' witch and don't appreciate inaccurate stereotypes. However, I have to concede that *Florence* matched all the fairy stories; she had the long gray hair and unorthodox appearance and you could never be sure of what she would say or do next. Both *Florence* and *Fred* behaved as if they were a digital thermometer short of a temperature drop and their abilities were questionable, even if their enthusiasm wasn't. *Florence* was always keen to remind everyone she met that she was a *bona fide* medium and probably the most accurate and genuine on the planet. No-one could honestly question *The Peabodys'* complete dedication to searching out the supernatural, but their methodology was, to my mind, somewhat questionable. Do remember what I've told you about *The Peabodys* as you work your way through this chapter: they are the only reason there is no photographic evidence of what happened to me at *Stately Manor*. They are a reminder to all to have several cameras and several photographers on any investigation.

After our short stop for a drink, we followed the directions we'd obtained from the locals in the pub, and wound our way along the road to our destination. Of course, *Stately Manor* is not the real name of our venue for this event, but I won't give that away as I would hate the current residents to suffer from a surfeit of ghost hunters appearing at their door in the middle of the night.

One often tends to think of manor houses as huge, sprawling affairs, but this is not always the case. Although small, *Stately Manor* is perfectly formed, with mullioned windows and a grand entrance, at which our hosts, *Lord and Lady Stately*, were waiting for us. Don't be fooled into thinking we were greeted by visions in tweed and plus fours - the *Statelys* were young, fun and genuinely interested in what we would do in their house. Having recently bought it, they had learned of its history and were keen to find out if there really was anything paranormal going on within its walls.

The interior of the house was furnished in a way that, surprisingly, suited it very well. It had everything you might expect of an eclectic manor house – and more besides. In the rabbit-warren of rooms you could find the mandatory stuffed fish and fowl alongside furniture from all ages (but none from a Swedish flat-pack manufacturer); a couple of sweeping stone staircases and a flattened warthog for a hearthrug.

The minute I walked into the house I felt at home. I loved it and everything about it. I could feel straight away that we were not alone there, but unusually this did not bother me and I settled in. I found that I was drawn to one particular staircase in the house, which started from the base of one of the biggest ground floor mullioned windows. I made myself comfortable a couple of steps up and admired the view. The more I looked at the view the less interested I was in the team and what we were there to do. The more I looked the more interested I was in what may come up the drive at any moment. It could be *him*! He may just be coming home now! I wanted to catch a glimpse of him riding up the drive, so that my heart could skip a beat before I opened the door to let him in. I was bursting to throw my arms around his neck and smother him in kisses.

And then – suddenly – back to reality. Who on earth was 'he'? I knew 'he' was handsome, with long dark hair and a goatee beard. I knew he was tanned and muscular and I knew I loved him with all my heart and soul. However, I also knew that I was single, lonely and here to hunt ghosts, and that knowledge brought me back to reality. I shook myself and went to look for the others.

Your love keeps lifting me higher

*'Gravity. It keeps you rooted to the ground. In space, there's not any
gravity. You just kind of leave your feet and go floating around. Is
that what being in love is like?'*
Josh Brand and John Falsey, *Northern Exposure* Pilot

I found part of our group in an area the Lord and Lady had
kindly set aside for smokers and, being someone afflicted with
the desire to fill their lungs with carcinogens myself, I joined
them. We sat and chatted, aware that the non-smokers were
working in another part of the building. It was not long before we
heard a scream from the other group in the house. Angela was
making a racket and the noise was coming from the room under
investigation.

'Di, get in here quick! He's here: you've *got* to feel him. Come
and help, quickly!'

I rushed to Angela's aid. I was absolutely astonished by the
scene that greeted me when I arrived in the investigation room.
Angela was in the middle of the room; but she was bent back
virtually horizontal, a few feet from the floor. Kerry and Michael
were trying to get her upright and struggling with the effort,
despite her slight physique.

'He's right there!' She pointed to the space in front of her. 'Get
in there Di, you'll feel him, he's really strong but he doesn't want
me!'

I obliged and stood in front of Angela. Kerry and Michael
continued to struggle manfully with Angela and the pressure on
her, but finally got her upright. She hastily retired to a seat along
the wall, well away from the spot where she had alleged 'he' was
standing.

As soon as I stood on that spot I felt a presence. It was not
unpleasant, but it was strong and very masculine. As I allowed
the presence to come closer I could see in my mind's eye (visions

are rare for me, as you probably already know) a really hunky Elizabethan gentleman. He had long brown hair; a goatee beard and a bronzed torso: which comprised of muscular arms, a flat stomach and an impressive six-pack. He was wearing intricately decorated white and gold breeches and had a gold and pearl earring in one ear. I believed that his name was Richard, but I cannot be sure that I heard this correctly: I had other things going on that were attracting my attention. I was sure, though, that he was the man that I had been waiting for when I sat on the stairs.

The team had been watching me closely. As well as Angela, Kerry and Michael, both of *The Peabodys* were in the room – with *Fred* sporting a camera. They were watching me intently, and Angela asked me what I was sensing. I didn't tell her about waiting for him on the stairs, but I did give her a little information about the man I could see.

As I recounted my impressions, I suddenly felt an arm snake around my waist. As I was the only one in the middle of the room apart from 'Richard', I knew the hand was his, but I felt totally at ease and did nothing to dissuade him. I continued to talk, while his other arm encircled me. To be honest, I really liked the feeling of being in a passionate embrace. I was at a stage in my life where I was single, lonely, sad and not really sure where I was going or what I would do in the future. Yes, sure, I knew that I was probably imagining this spirit man and of course, I knew full well that his attentions were probably a product of my longing, but frankly – I didn't care.

When he started kissing up my neck, I was pretty sure I was hallucinating. The team asked me what else I was picking up and I brushed them off saying that I was still 'tuning in'. The kissing got very much more passionate and I could feel both love and lust from his presence. I was flattered and really quite enjoying the sensations; so I continued to tell my friends that I was tuning in and didn't give them any clue that I was being seduced by a spook. Despite the fact that Richard was at least 500 years my senior, I was prepared to ignore the age difference and concentrate on the very immediate certainty that he was genuinely attracted to me and that he was single. Couple that with the fact that there would be no need to cook for him; clean for him or clear up after him: in my opinion, the potential for a rewarding relationship was enormous!

'Richard' pulled me backwards against his chest and continued kissing my neck. I was really enjoying feeling loved and desired again and had quite lost myself to it, when *Marcus* came rushing into the room.

'My God, it's a scene from *The Exorcist*!' he exclaimed.

Marcus looked really shocked at what he was witnessing on his arrival. His outburst shocked me too; and it was then that I noticed everyone else staring at me, some with their mouths wide open. I focused my attention away from Richard's passionate kisses and asked *Marcus* just what he meant.

As *Marcus* tried to explain why he was so surprised, the penny dropped. Yes, Richard was very real to me, I could physically feel him. From where I was standing it would be fair to say to say that using the vernacular 'stiff' for his spirit would not be an exaggeration. However, no-one else could see him and they were not aware of everything that was happening to me. The only thing they could see was me. As you may remember, Richard's embrace included him pulling me back against his chest. This resulted in me leaning on him fully, which was a perfectly comfortable place to be as far as I was concerned. To the team watching me, it was not comfortable at all. All they could see was my body leaning at an angle to the floor that defied the laws of gravity and should have resulted in me falling down hard on my back!

Thank goodness *The Peabodys* had a camera and were busy taking photos while this was going on! What a shame though, that these photos (as I later discovered – to my horror) were all of my head and shoulders. *The Peabodys* had not taken *any* of my full body showing the impossible angle I was leaning at! Perhaps now you can understand why they were not considered the brightest torches in the flight case?

The shock of what the team were witnessing brought me round: that and the fact that Richard and his passion was becoming a bit too much. He may have been long dead, but his ardor most definitely wasn't. Being human and celibate for way too long, neither was mine. I had to end what could have been a beautiful and uncomplicated relationship by cutting my connection with him, because the game was well and truly up. The team wanted to know what had happened to me psychically that had prompted the physical response they had seen: and they wanted to know now.

So I told them. Yes, I may have missed out a few of the more unbelievable details, but I explained how I felt a real connection to Richard and that although there was definitely passion, I also felt love…of sorts at least. I admitted that I thought it was all my imagination, but was reassured by the crew that they knew there was truth in what I had said. They had seen the amazing physical phenomena (my position in a gravity-defying slant above the floor) while I was interacting with him.

The Hand of Fatima

'Time is an illusion. Lunchtime doubly so.'
Douglas Adams, author, 1952–2001

Needless to say, we were all intrigued by my encounter with Richard and wanted to know if there was any background to support the story. The answer to that is 'maybe'. Legend has it that *Stately Manor* was home to a member of the landed gentry called Ralph, whose ancestors had lived there since the 15th Century. He was betrothed to a young lady called Fatima.

Ralph, being a loyal subject of the crown, heeded the call to arms when Richard the Lionheart decided to start the crusades and duly went off to fight the heathens. During his time abroad, he met the daughter of a Saracen, and was unfaithful to Fatima. Even sadder, Fatima died before Ralph returned from the crusades and her broken-hearted spirit is said to haunt *Stately Manor*.

There is another version of the story (which I like better) which says that Fatima was a daughter of the Saracens. When her lover Ralph left to go home, Fatima followed him, but she sadly died on her journey to England. Her spirit is said to wait for Ralph at his home, and sometimes plays a harp in the grounds, hoping the music may hurry him to her.

Long Lost Love?

"Tis the most tender part of love, each other to forgive.'
John Sheffield, English statesman, poet and the 1st Duke of Buckingham and Normanby, 1647–1721

Did I pick up the love and longing of Fatima? Was Richard actually Ralph, still consumed with the original passion he had for Fatima? Was he trying to let her know he still loved her, despite his infidelity? Or was I really just very lonely and very flexible in my attitude towards gravity? These questions and more will forever haunt me and I have often wished that Richard (or Ralph), would do so too.

I will probably never know who 'Richard' was or why he chose me to express his unfulfilled passion. However, I do know that I have, like probably everyone else on the planet, harbored longings for people I couldn't have – and imagined myself with them. I also know that these fantasies might have been fun, but they have never been as vivid as the one I had at *Stately Manor*.

I won't forget *Stately Manor* and its incumbent ghost. It would be hard to do so. I now live just a few miles away from where the manor still stands and I have finally found a living equivalent of Richard. The path that I have meandered along before settling in this part of the UK has been convoluted and full of challenges. It is a small miracle – and in my opinion one hell of a coincidence – to find myself living so close to the place where I had felt enveloped in true love (not to mention a good dollop of passion as well). Combine that with the fact that my living 'Richard' lives in the same area as *Stately Manor* and questions about the workings of Fate raise their heads. Maybe I should learn to play the harp and see what happens when my own 'Richard' hears it?

'Death ends a life, not a relationship.'
Jack Lemmon, actor, 1925–2001

Witch Life is That?

'In the cool of the evening, they used to gather,
'neath the stars in the meadow circling an old oak tree.
At the times appointed by the seasons of the earth and the phases of
the moon.
In the center, often stood a woman, equal with the others respected
for her word.
One of the many they call the witches, the healers and the teachers
of the wisdom of the Earth.'
Christy Moore, *The Burning Times*

Of all the past life experiences I've had, the one I lived through alone in my own shop was probably the weirdest, if not the most thought-provoking.

All my life I have believed in some divine power, some God, and had never questioned His or Her existence, just the nature that that existence took. My interest in the nature of divinity had led me to read copious amounts of literature on a number of faiths and mystical traditions. I found myself drawn again and again to witchcraft or, as it is often called nowadays, Wicca. Despite the tendency to gravitate towards the term 'Wicca', Witchcraft and Wicca seem to be interchangeable terms. I have no desire to debate which witch is which, so for the sake of continuity, I have used the terms 'Witch' and 'Witchcraft'.

One with Nature

'Nature is just enough; but men and women must comprehend and accept Her suggestions.'
Antoinette Brown Blackwell, the first woman to be ordained as a minister in the United States, 1825–1921

For those of you unfamiliar with the religious beliefs of witches or, more importantly, for those of you who are misinformed about Witchcraft, I would like to set down a few basic tenets of the faith, so that you can follow this story with a clearer understanding of my motivations and goals and hopefully understand it better. Please do take on board that the following interpretation of Witchcraft is mine. Every witch will have his or her own interpretation and that is, in my humble opinion, as it should be.

Witchcraft is a nature-based religion that comes under the umbrella of Paganism. A Witch is to Paganism as a Methodist is to Christianity – just one branch of a very large tree. Witchcraft came to prominence in 1954 when Gerald Gardner, a retired civil servant, became interested in magick (the 'k' is added to 'magic' to differentiate from conjuror's tricks). He investigated a number of mystical practices and then extracted Witchcraft from them, which he said was a modern interpretation of the ancient pagan faith that predates Christianity.

The origins of Witchcraft cannot be proven, but many nations have folklore that implies the existence of a pagan faith similar in nature to Gardner's Witchcraft – and the stories date back many hundreds of years. Pagan ceremonies such as well-dressing, Maypole dancing and 'Obby 'Oss riding are part of Western heritage despite being centuries old – and they still continue in many places today.

Gardnerian Witchcraft is very distinct in its practices and still has a considerable following. It requires that members belong to a coven (a group of witches that worship together) and that they are initiated in a ritualistic fashion. There are other coven-based faiths: Alexandrian Witchcraft being another prominent example. Despite the variations, there are some central beliefs that apply to all types of witchcraft. Before you assume any stereotype, let me assure you that human and/or animal sacrifice is NOT part of witchcraft.

Which Witch?

I am a solitary witch. I am very eclectic and am also quite comfortable with Christianity, which appears to be uncommon amongst witches. You may think I am hedging my bets because I will wear a cross or a pentagram; but the truth is that I believe that there are many paths up the same mountain and I am happy to acknowledge most of them. Not all witches practice as solitaries; there are many covens that thrive in all parts of the world, each with their own style.

Contrary to popular belief, Witchcraft is not anti-Christian. It is simply *not* Christian, just different. Another misconception is that Witchcraft is connected with Satanism. It isn't: Witches do not believe in a devil figure, so it would be very hard for them to worship one! I am not sure about a devil myself, although I *am* sure about the evil that one can find if one goes looking for it – and the easiest place to find it is among the living!

What Witches Do

> '*Everyone ought to worship God according to his own inclinations, and not to be constrained by force.*'
> Flavius Josephus, Jewish priest and scholar, 37AD–100AD

Yep, you're right, witches do perform magick. Magick is simply a form of praying or celebrating certain times of year and does not involve living sacrifices. Witchcraft is a duotheistic religion, where both a God and Goddess are worshiped as opposite sides of the same coin. I believe in the coin as a whole (one omnipotent force) as well as the two sides; but many witches will focus their faith entirely on the God and Goddess. Witchcraft is closely connected to nature and natural forces. The God and Goddess are seen in all things, but perhaps seen clearer in the wilds of nature, where their full power is potent and real.

What Witches Are

- As a solitary Witch I work; cook for my family; pay the bills; clean the toilet and have a shower...just like you do.

- I don't wear odd clothes as a rule and I only wear black because it's slimming.

- I do have a wart, but this is a recent addition courtesy of Old Father Time and looks more like a birthmark.

- My hair *is* long: but it's clean and black as opposed to the expected gray (thank you to the nice people who make hair colorants!).

- I don't ride a broom for transport, I have a *Kia Picanto*. I use my broom to sweep the kitchen.

- I don't have a (living) cat; I'm mildly allergic to them.

- I absolutely love garlic.

- Running water is not a problem. I often do a very bad impression of the Wicked Witch of the West from the *Wizard of Oz* if I cross a very large river, though. This is for effect and *not* because I'm melting.

- I do like candles, moonlight, traditional folklore and the countryside.

- I am nice to animals and nice to my fellow man.

In essence, Witches are just people. They have the same problems that everyone has and their lifestyles match their circumstances – just as yours does. You would not be able to spot a witch in the street simply by looking at them. Their reverence for nature can be a giveaway and in some cases the exclamation 'Oh my Goddess!' might be a clue; but other than that they look, behave and live as you do. They worship differently and that's about it.

Shopping for Witches

'When, however, one reads of a witch being ducked, of a woman possessed by devils, of a wise woman selling herbs, or even a very remarkable man who had a mother, then I think we are on the track of a lost novelist, a suppressed poet...indeed, I would venture to guess that Anon, who wrote so many poems without signing them, was often a woman.'
Virginia Woolf, novelist, diarist and feminist, 1882 - 1941

I am sure you've all heard about the persecution of witches in days gone by, and of the burnings, hangings, drownings and torture that took place. We have records that prove that many old women were put to horrific deaths after being accused of worshiping the Devil, which our ancestors believed was a tenet of witchcraft. I had always felt incensed that some little old ladies that were disliked by their neighbors suffered horribly for no justifiable reason. I am quite outspoken in my opinion that religious tolerance is crucial for the good of all.

Therefore, when I had the opportunity to start a business; I opted to open a Pagan shop in York, England, so that others who followed alternative faiths could find a place to buy items they needed. It was a risky venture opening a Pagan shop in York – where the Minster, York's stunning gothic cathedral, stands proud as a testimony to the all-encompassing nature of Christianity – but I did it nonetheless.

I would like to put it on record that in my time as a shop owner in York, I did not experience any intolerance or hatred from Christians. In fact; many of them were kind, considerate, and customers. I was more than happy to stock rosaries and crucifixes along with bells, books and candles and this may have had something to do with the response that I received from the Christian element of the population. York Christians seemed to be very Christian in their attitude. The only trouble I ever had was from some pot-smoking miscreants who broke my shop windows and stole some items for drug money – they were never apprehended, more's the pity.

Every morning when I came in to open up the shop to the public, I had a set routine. I would arrive; put some coffee on so that I could offer customers a cup; say a few prayers; light some incense; and open my emails and deal with them. I would then open the shop.

This one morning, I was running late. As you will already know if you've read this far, I don't 'do' late. I rushed into my shop, went through my usual routine with some haste, but only got as far as clicking on the emails to see what was in. There was a mail from my online tutor – and I always read that in peace before the shop opened.

Spiritual tutors are something special. If you find your own tutor (and the best ones are found by accident) then you will doubtless develop a very close bond. This bond is one that many may interpret as more than friendship, including the person being taught. It is a bond that goes above attraction in reality; it is not about earthly delights, but more about spiritual connection. When that connection is first felt it can be confusing.

It is no surprise then that my tutor, whom I shall refer to as *Michael*, was very important to me and his emails were always intriguing and special. Our online relationship, which was tutor to pupil, was often misconstrued as something more by others around us. Because of people's misunderstanding of the situation, I made a point of not speaking to him by phone unless there was a very good reason.

Despite the fact that there was an email from *Michael*, time was pressing. I remember that I clicked to open the email, saw that it was an awful lot of prose, and closed it immediately as I didn't have time to read it properly. I got up and opened the shop, just in time to make sure that I stuck to my advertised opening hours.

Once I was sure that all was well, I poured myself a coffee and settled down to read my emails, with the one from *Michael* being top of the list. Yet again, I was thwarted in reading it. Not by a customer, sadly, but by a sudden explosion in my head accompanied by a very powerful vision. I was plunged headlong into another lifetime.

The Burning Times

'It is curious that physical courage should be so common in the world and moral courage so rare.'
Mark Twain, author and humorist, 1835 - 1910

I found myself in the middle of a crowd. In front of me, there was a throng of the unwashed masses. They were baying and jeering: in my opinion they were the epitome of an angry mob. Needless to say when I couldn't see any pitchforks I felt really let down. As you'll now know, I do hold the firm belief that angry mobs should always have pitchforks. So far I've been hugely disappointed whenever I've 'seen' one…but I digress.

Looking through the angry mob, I could see a man, tied to a stake. He was surrounded by a huge pile of brushwood, and I could hear someone near him reciting a litany of accusations. The crowd was calling for his blood, but I only know this because I could feel it, not because I could understand them. Everyone was talking in a strange language, and I could not make it out properly. However, although I did not recognize the tongue the people were speaking, I did know what they were saying.

As I looked, I realized that I knew the man tied to the stake. The man was my lover – and I had accused him of witchcraft. That was why he was tied to the stake and why he was about to be burnt to death. I also knew that the reason I had accused him was because I had originally been accused of the same crime myself. I was a coward. An accusation of witchcraft was a guarantee you would be executed – unless you could suggest someone else who was more deserving of the punishment.

As that realization came to me, I saw the officials light the pyre. I saw the flames leap up, and caught the eye of the man who was about to die a horrible death. He just looked sad. The flames crept higher, and I could start to smell his flesh crisp. Nausea overcame me, but I looked on, unable to tear my eyes away from the gruesome scene before me. The fire continued to burn, and it was only when I was sure that he had died that I found myself back in my chair with my still full cup of coffee in my hand.

Karma, not calmer

I felt a wreck. The vision had been so incredibly real, and the look in the eyes of the burning man coupled with the smell, the sound and the sight of his death had torn at my very soul. It had reached into my heart, ripped it out and stomped on it. It was not being witness to this most gruesome sight that was killing me; it was the fact that I had, in quite a direct way, been responsible for his death. To add insult to horrific injury, I also knew that the man in the scene had reincarnated and was now my tutor, but that I was seeing him many centuries before, in one of his previous incarnations. This probably sounds a bit far-fetched to you, but I *knew* it. I didn't need proof – every part of me was completely sure that it was fact. If you think the story so far is weird, believe me, it gets weirder!

I was really, really distressed by what I had experienced. So distressed, I decided to call *Michael*. I was in luck, as he answered the phone very promptly. I attempted to tell him what had happened and how sorry I was for what I had done, but he just said 'So you've read my email, then?' I faltered. Here I was, desperately trying to apologize for the most incredible display of cowardice and selfishness, and all he was trying to do was to find out what I thought of his email!

Crying, I tried again to tell him what had happened. Again, he referred to his email. I tried one more time, and this time he took the hint. He let me finish, and then told me that I should go away and read his email, and that if I still had something I wanted to say to him I could call back – but that everything was ok now.

Still very distressed, I did as he asked. There was the email winking at me, still unread. I clicked it open and started to read. It seemed very boring to start off with; some comments about a man and his life, seemingly unconnected with anything we had studied and not of a great deal of interest. Then it got much more interesting. The man in the email was dying. He was tied to a stake, watching his lover as flames engulfed his body. The email described the scene from the man's point of view and commented more on his sadness at the betrayal by his lover than on the incredible pain that he must have been experiencing. Then it ended.

I freaked. I honestly, completely and totally freaked out. I didn't know where to put myself and what to do. I wanted to phone him, then I didn't; then I wanted to go home and drink copious amounts of alcohol; then I wanted to run off and become a nun. I couldn't think straight and my coffee grew skin. *My* skin crawled all over my body in a desperate attempt to move to somewhere that was a lot calmer.

Finally, I did phone him. He was very non-committal, saying he was pleased that I'd finally found out for myself about our past connection and saying that it was all over now. He said he didn't harbor any ill-will and that it would all work out. He didn't, at any point, explain how he *knew* what I was going to experience, or about our past lives. If you knew *Michael*, you wouldn't have asked him, anyway. He could just do that sort of thing, and knowing him, even virtually, meant that every act was one where you wondered if there was someone other than a deity watching you.

Adjusting the Balance

'We can be sure that the greatest hope for maintaining equilibrium in the face of any situation rests within ourselves.'
Francis J Braceland, *O magazine*, April 2003

It was some months later that all the tiny pieces fell into place. I realized why I had always compared myself to the disciple Peter (not because of my saintliness, I hasten to add); always assuming instinctively that I would be the one denying Jesus if my own life was on the line. I figured out why I had always considered myself a coward; even though no-one had ever called me one and I had not done anything that would be considered cowardly. I also realized why I was so determined to stand up for religious tolerance and understood that where I was at that moment was exactly where I should be.

In 1951, *The Witchcraft Act* of the UK was finally repealed. This superstitious piece of parliamentary nonsense, which imprisoned people for alleging to summon spirits and the like, was replaced with *The Fraudulent Mediums Act*. This law was an attempt to ensure that the public were protected from the machinations of con artists, alleging to use psychic powers to fleece people of large sums of money. Today it has been repealed and replaced by the *Fraudulent Mediums Act 2008* that makes all mediums traders who offer a commodity. Their readings are regulated as a consumer product. This is all a bit nonsensical to me, but I guess the public have to be protected from charlatans somehow. I just hope it is not a subtle way of bringing back the burnings!

2001 was the fiftieth anniversary of the abolishment of *The Witchcraft Act*, and it was 2001 right now and I had already planned to do something to celebrate our country's move towards some sort of tolerance towards alternative faiths. I had planned the unveiling of a plaque (which I sponsored the majority of) and I had been desperately trying to get an Anglican Vicar and a High Priestess of Witchcraft to unveil it together: to demonstrate that the past could be put behind us and we could live together in harmony, if not in total agreement.

Again, I'll have to reiterate that the people of York, a city that very much symbolizes the success of Christianity, were very Christian in their attitude towards my request to find a Vicar or Priest. I'm *not* being sarcastic: I spoke to many clergy and although they were bound to refuse, they were very kind indeed and wished me well in my quest. I finally contacted Chaplain David Hart from Derby, who was a strong supporter of *Interfaith* – people from different faiths who come together as a community to attempt to understand and work together. He agreed to unveil the plaque along with Kate West, a well-known High Priestess of Witchcraft.

The event went off without a hitch and with a great turn out for the march we took through York City center and down to York Dungeon. Here the plaque was put up and subsequently unveiled in the Witchcraft exhibit. Kate and David got on like a house on fire and joined the rest of us for a sociable drink at a local bar. I was so very happy; I had always wanted to see two (allegedly) opposing faiths standing side-by-side to encourage tolerance of all faiths. My dream had come true. Not only that: I also felt as if a burden had been lifted…and my mind went back to my past life as a coward, watching my lover burn. I felt as if I had, to some degree, appeased Karma and hoped and prayed that more people would realize that it is our differences that make us special. As long as we are kind to each other, the God or Goddess we pray to will smile kindly on us.

'Everyone has the right to freedom of thought, conscience and religion; this right includes freedom to change his religion or belief, and freedom, either alone or in community with others and in public or private, to manifest his religion or belief in teaching, practice, worship and observance.'
Article 18, Universal Declaration of Human Rights
(Adopted and proclaimed by General Assembly resolution 217 A (III) of 10 December 1948)
Words on the plaque unveiled in York Dungeon in 2001.

Have You Lived Before?

I expect you will be wondering if you have lived before. No-one can prove you have, but then again, no-one can prove you haven't. It takes belief, and perhaps experience.

Past Life Regression (or Past Life Therapy, which is regression for a reason other than curiosity) can be helpful. Regression is mentioned as a working technique in the *Upanishads* of ancient India, but was brought to prominence by the infamous Madame Blavatsky – co-founder of *The Theosophical Society*.

Both Past Life Regression and Past Life Therapy use hypnosis to help the individual to access memories of what are believed to be previous lives (often referred to by Buddhists as 'incarnations'). Some hypnotists specialize in this area – my friend Carole Chui being one of these. There are also many unqualified hypnotherapists out there and I would recommend that you give them a wide berth, no matter how well-intentioned and practiced they are.

Even after a really deep and enlightening regression it is really difficult to be sure if you have lived before. If you are looking for conclusive proof, I do not believe you will find it. What you might find, however, could change your outlook on life for the better. It certainly has for me.

What does one experience during a regression?

This is the most commonly asked question about regression and it is also the one where the most assumptions are made. Usually, the hypnotist will lead the subject into a very relaxed state and use suggestion to help them to access a past life. No special equipment is needed, just a comfortable chair or couch and no interruptions by phone calls or door bells.

When the hypnotist is satisfied that the subject is relaxed and has reached an appropriate point in their session, a series of questions will be asked and the hypnotist will record the experiences the subject recounts. Making notes of the session also helps the subject to recall what they experienced when they return to normal waking consciousness.

Not all subjects go into their past lives fully cognizant of that life: not all subjects 'live it'. I am someone who only reaches a very light level of awareness and, as you can probably tell from this chapter, that is more than enough for me to be pretty convinced I had lived that life.

In general, hypnosis subjects can reach one of three levels:

- **Superficial Trance**: the lightest stage, where the subject is still consciously aware of their surroundings and environment but also aware of where their 'other self' is.

- **The Alpha Stage**: a deeper stage where the breathing and heart rate slows down and the subject is more keenly aware of their past life surroundings and only lightly aware of their modern self.

- **Complete Trance**: where the subject has fully realized their past life self and is completely living that experience.

It is a fallacy that you have to reach the third stage to get anything out of a Past Life Regression.

Have you always been afraid of the sea, but don't know why? Maybe you drowned in a past life? Accessing this life could cure you of this fear for good. Maybe you have an unusual birthmark? Was this an injury from a past life? There are all sorts of things you can learn and release, but this type of therapy will only work when you are 'ready', which is why you must take precautions to seek out professionals. If you do decide to try to find out who you were, may your search prove fruitful and may your results prove positively life-changing!

Chapter 7
Possession

'A man's real possession is his memory. In nothing else is he rich, in nothing else is he poor.'
Alexander Smith, Scottish essayist and poet, 1830–1867

When people talk of experiences with ghosts, very few will tell you they've been possessed. And yet, most people who don't ghost hunt (or haven't seen a ghost), seem to be very afraid of this concept; as if it may happen to them at any moment. Perhaps this is because of the vast amount of literature and films available on the subject; or maybe it's the rapid increase in ghost hunting programs, most of which seem to have possession as a regular occurrence. I don't know why people believe that possession happens so often, but from my experience they do, and they are mortally afraid of it.

Before I start to tell you of the few 'possession' experiences I have had, I would like to tell you first of all that possession is rare...very, very rare. Complete possession – where a Spirit takes you over entirely and you are powerless to behave in any way other than in ways they want you to – is unknown to me. I have been 'possessed', but even in the most extreme circumstances I've always had some control and have always come out of it unscathed.

As a medium, I am going to be a better target for Spirit Possession than someone who isn't: I'm already attuned to the

Spirits' frequency. If you go looking for trouble you will probably find it, so don't go looking! Even if you do, it is still extremely unlikely that you will be taken over and be unable to do anything about it. It is very hard for any spirit to manifest – let alone take someone over – so you can put thoughts of possession out of your mind. There is a much higher likelihood that you will have a lower tax bill this year than there is that you will become possessed.

The Hag of Netley Abbey

'I envy people who drink. At least they have something to blame everything on.'
Oscar Levant, composer and author, 1906–1972

So having told you that the chance of possession is very slim, I will now tell you about the time that I had a very up-front and personal contact with a spirit at Netley Abbey.

Netley Abbey is a wonderful building, not far from Portsmouth. It was founded in 1239 by Peter des Roches, the Bishop of Winchester. Home to the Cistercian order of monks it was one of a pair of Abbeys, the other being in France. It is maintained by *English Heritage*, who do a sterling job, but rarely let ghost hunters explore the buildings in their care. Therefore, I was very lucky to get the chance to wander the ruins of the Abbey at night, and even luckier that the group I was with were alone in the building. Unfortunately, my mood meant that I was not feeling lucky at the time.

Yet again, I was the designated driver for our trip to Netley. Many of our group had decided that this was more a trip for fun than anything else, so they intended to have a drink or two on the way. I feel very strongly about drinking and ghost hunting: why would you believe any data or experience from a ghost hunt if the person providing it had been under the influence? Certainly I didn't want to drink if I was ghost hunting, and as the driver there was no way I would have anything except a juice. Probably only one juice at that, as there were not going to be any toilets readily available in a ruin.

Despite the fact that I didn't want to drink, I did feel miffed that I had got lumbered with the driving again. It seemed to me that I was always driving and there were other drivers going on this particular occasion. However, I put up with it, even though I was tired from a lot of driving the day before and would have preferred to have an early night.

We left our rendezvous point in a car which I had never driven. The trip was interesting to say the least, especially as the Vodka had already been opened by those in the back of the vehicle. Let me introduce you to the team.

Firstly there was *Marcus,* whom you've already come across. He was one of the first to start on the sauce and was in high spirits. This meant that I was bound to have a bad time, as he would use me as a whipping boy for anything that didn't go *just* right, in his not-so-humble opinion.

Then there was Norie. Norie Miles is a really experienced, dedicated ghost investigator with a wealth of experience and a real passion for what she does. She was also having a drink or two, but don't be fooled – under normal circumstances, Norie takes ghost investigation extremely seriously and is totally professional. Norie I can forgive for having a drink: she works hard and, on this occasion, she deserved to play hard too.

Lee and Kevin were also with us for the night. Lee provided the vehicle for our trip and was also experienced at ghost investigation. Kevin didn't have a lot of experience in the field, but was hugely passionate about learning and was a good friend of *Marcus's* at the time. As with most of *Marcus's* friends, that didn't last.

We also had Paul Ig; Paul H and Marian. If you include me along with these three, you have the full mediumistic complement, with the team mentioned in the previous paragraphs acting as the guys with the equipment. Paul H and Marian have worked professionally as mediums and are well respected for their talents. Paul Ig had also used his mediumistic skills before. I would note that all of the mediums were sober for the duration of the night.

Eventually, after a stop to refuel (the drinkers in the team, not the car), we arrived at Netley Abbey and met up with the guardians to get access. We left the car in the car park and walked across the grounds to the ruins. All the way there I was moaning. I really didn't want to do this at all, I was tired, fed up and had already been treated abominably by *Marcus*, who had virtually ignored me when he was holding court in the pub we'd stopped at, but treated me as a servant if he'd needed something.

After a short trudge we reached the entrance to the Abbey ruins. I had walked across the grounds with Paul H and Marian, as much to see what they picked up as to avoid *Marcus*. I didn't want to be at the Abbey, but if I had to be there I wanted to do an investigation properly. As we crossed the threshold to the Abbey, I immediately felt sick. I do mean immediately, it was like a switch had been turned on – one minute fine, the next, sick. I managed to hold back the nausea, and noticed that both Marian and Paul H had felt it too. Once they had got over their attack of sickness, Marian and Paul H exclaimed that they could see hundreds of spirits in the parapets on top of the walls. I took pictures where they said, and each picture had an orb on it at the point they had indicated. This proved nothing, of course, but it was certainly very interesting and at the very least, a surprising coincidence.

From the open part of the ruins we made our way further inside, where there were some part-rooms and some that were still intact. The nausea became more tolerable and I stopped worrying about embarrassing myself and / or redecorating the interior of the Abbey. It was in an intact room, the Infirmary, where we conducted our first experiment: recording for an EVP.

Electronic Voice Phenomena explained

EVP stands for Electronic Voice Phenomena. Attempting to pick up EVP is a popular technique with paranormal investigators. In 1959, a film producer called Friedrich Jürgenson was out recording bird song for a program he was producing. When he got home and reviewed the tape (which was reel-to-reel) he was amazed to discover what sounded like his father's voice, in between the bird noises. His father had died some time ago. Chronologically further along the tape, he alleged he could hear his dead wife calling him. After discovering these strange noises that could not be heard at the time of recording, he went on to make other recordings to see if the mysterious voices were ever heard again. He was not disappointed. On one tape he maintained that he received a message from his mother.

Since Jürgenson's time, EVP production has become more sophisticated and incorporated the latest technology. At the time of our EVP session, the equipment of choice was a digital recorder, the type you may use for dictation. Having a digital recorder meant that there was no chance of a stretched cassette tape mimicking odd sounds and no chance that a prior recording on that tape could come through – because there was no tape.

There are two commonly-used methods to EVP attempts. One of them is to record a place in complete silence, leaving the recorder running in a room that is locked and free from draughts or the entrance of insects. The second method is the one that the group and I used and the one that I have used most often since: to ask questions of any resident spirits and to leave a silence in between the questions for the spirits to answer.

Is Anybody There?

'I wish people who have trouble communicating would just shut up.'
Tom Lehrer – singer / songwriter and satirist

I had always maintained that I would never be totally convinced by EVP unless I had seen the whole thing set up from start to finish and been there throughout. I had said that I would also need to see that there was no chance of outside noise creeping in. Netley Abbey has extensive grounds; the nearest someone could get to the place (unless they were inside) would be walking along the path that surrounded the grounds. Anyone walking outside would be way too far away for us to hear, even if they were shouting.

Paul Ig set up the EVP. The whole group was in the room at the time, and although some members of the team were slightly merry by now, there was complete silence while the questions were asked.

We listened to the playback. There were some noises on it, but we all felt that they may have been there before, and were not convinced. So, the machine was passed over to *Marcus,* who set it up while Paul Ig filmed.

I thought we'd need several attempts to get a noise from spirit, even a noise that someone could misinterpret while drunk. I thought we'd have even more attempts and then still get nothing that any sober member of the team would think was unusual. I waited smugly, my annoyance at being present making me usefully cynical. I was completely wrong about what I thought would happen.

The playback sounded like this:

'Is there anyone there who wishes to communicate with us?'

...pause

'Can you tell us your name?'

...pause

'Can you tell us what year it is?'

We all heard *Marcus* ask the questions. As we started to listen to the playback, we could still hear him saying them, but couldn't hear anything else. That was, until *Marcus* asked the question about what year it was. Much to everyone's surprise in the room

– and to my absolute abject horror – a deep, elderly male voice stated "73' in response to that question.

Marcus was so shocked at the response on the dictation machine he threw the machine on the floor! As one, the rest of the team inhaled deeply and I could see a number of jaws drop. However, we all kept quiet as the recording continued.

'Is there anything we can do to help you?'

The same elderly male voice responded and his response tore at my heart strings, despite my fear.

'Please help me...please?'

I think I have already explained how I feel about being scared. I don't like it, I react badly to it and I try to avoid it (yes, maybe ghost hunting is a strange way of avoiding it). Fight and flight mechanisms normally argue and I stand there shaking and hyperventilating. As soon as I heard this final comment from the mysterious voice, fight and flight decided to stop arguing and just leave altogether. Presumably they were heading for a convenient bar, where they wouldn't have to try to work anything out and could just sit and have a beer instead. I created my own mantra to deal with the very real fear that I was experiencing, as my normal reactions had taken a vacation. It went something like this:

'I want to go home'; it continued with the line 'I want to go home' and was finally followed by the plea: 'I want to go home'.

After the play-back, the team decided to move to the Abbot's lodge. In this room, another EVP was set up. Again, there was complete silence during the set up. I stuck to reciting my mantra in my head and I made sure that I only shook silently.

I had thought that hearing a voice respond was the scariest thing that could possibly happen on an EVP. I was wrong again. Sometimes, it's not what is said, but *how* it is said...

The recording was played back and all seemed well to me; there were no responses. That is, there were no responses until the recording reached the end of the final question (asking if we could help the spirit in any way). The voice on the dictation machine was nothing like the gentle but sad male voice that had responded earlier. This voice sounded like it came from the pits of Hell – assuming Hell is full of voices that can chill you to the bone. Crossed between a growl and a snarl, the voice said, simply, '*Leave!*'

I started reciting my mantra out loud now, desperately wanting the others to listen to the wisdom inherent in its carefully thought-out words; but everyone else was distracted. 'This is interesting!' and 'Pass the Vodka!' were the only comments I received. Several other attempts were made with the digital recorder, and other equipment was used too, but nothing of any consequence was recorded.

Witness Statement
'Since a child I have been visiting Netley Abbey, as a child ghost hunter with my parents, and then on my own or with friends as the years passed.
'The night I was there with Diana, we were in the Infirmary to do our first EVP, which to this day must be the best audible I have ever encountered. The voice was loud and clear, not like the usual ones. Normally you have to listen to an EVP a dozen times to work out what it is saying, as it is so quiet. The EVPs that night did shock me, especially with what happened to Diana later ...'
Norie Miles, ghost investigator, *Out There Media*

Unnatural Noises
We left the room; I was still reciting my mantra. The group then moved to another location, which was also under cover and had a small hole that led through to another room. I'd love to describe the small room through the hole, but I can't as I wouldn't go into that room for love nor money. The moment we reached the entrance I felt sick and backed away. Some of the less sober members of our team decided they'd go in for a laugh.

They didn't laugh.

Marcus went in first, followed by Norie and Kevin. Kevin was first out, though. Maybe my sickness was very contagious and quick-acting, maybe he'd drunk too much. Whatever the reason, Kevin rushed out of the hole and was promptly sick. As we gave Kevin some much-needed space, we waited for Norie and *Marcus* to appear. As we waited, we started to feel uneasy, and then the reason for our unease became apparent. It was one of the strangest sounds I've ever heard; it sounded like a rushing wind and then became a scream. The source of the sound was obvious to all of us – it came from the room that Norie and *Marcus* were in. Needless to say, they came out pretty smartly after that. They assured us they didn't make the sound, but we didn't need much assurance, as it was obvious it was not a sound that could be delivered by a living human being.

A Thing Possessed

'What sane person could live in this world and not be crazy?'
Ursula K. LeGuin – American science fiction writer

The team all seemed in good spirits, despite the horrible noise and the disturbing EVP. I wasn't, but you'll know that already. As most of the team went off to study another part of the building, I made some excuses and moved away a little, accompanied by Paul Ig. Sadly, I had not moved far enough away, as I was soon to find out.

Paul Ig and I chatted. I complained a lot too; but he was very understanding. We talked about mediumship and ghost investigation, as well as putting the world to rights in general. I felt a lot better for the break from the investigation and I relaxed. Perhaps that was my mistake, I don't know.

As we continued to talk, a noise drew our attention, a noise that came from the same area as the scream. Again, I could hear the sound of rushing wind, but it did not have a scream attached: the noise that came with it was impossible to describe, but sounded vaguely human. We both heard it and looked at each other as it came closer. I remember I felt as if I was rooted to the spot, but these events were probably a lot quicker in the happening than they are happening in the telling.

Suddenly, the noise was upon us; or, more accurately, was upon me. I was saying something to Paul Ig about the noise and was quite sound and sober in my statement and demeanor, until the noise 'hit'. Once it had reached me, I starting sobbing uncontrollably, and gibbering. I know I did, because a part of me seemed to be watching the rest of me, and the rest of me was now inhabited by an alien presence: a presence that was stark, staring mad.

I could feel 'her' sharing my space, I could feel her pain and her confusion and I also felt powerless to do anything. I seemed to have no choice but to let her cry and gibber, while for all the world it looked like it was me that was crying and gibbering.

Fortunately, Paul Ig is a medium, and he was well aware that I was not alone. I struggled to shake off this woman; at least I think she was a woman, I couldn't be sure as the effect of her presence was so intense. It was not easy. I felt as if she was just going to make my body cry and gibber forever. Fortunately, between my mental efforts and Paul's, I shook her off and returned to my 'normal' self: terrified. I started to talk to Paul about the experience and managed to get some straightforward sentences out before...she struck again. Yet again I was thrust away from myself and the wailing, sobbing, gibbering wreck took over.

I have already told you that I was not happy about being at the site, but I was stone-cold sober and in complete control of my senses before the hag jumped me. I'm not attention-seeking enough to rant and rave when I can't get my own way; the crying and gibbering did not come from me. What was happening to me was inexplicable as far as I was concerned, I knew there was a presence with me and I knew it was not my imagination. Paul Ig also felt this presence and was doing his best to help me.

Paul and I were attempting to remove the hag for the second time when the rest of the team returned. They were laughing and joking and waving a photo they'd taken that they alleged was ectoplasm. They seemed in high spirits. I wasn't. I was upset and scared and I'd had enough. I told them in no uncertain terms that this was the last straw and I was leaving. If they wanted to get home they had better come too, because I was taking the car and leaving Netley Abbey as fast as I safely could. I stuck to my word.

Witness Statement (...cont.)

'... Netley has always been my favourite location to investigate as it never seems to disappoint for phenomena. The night I was there with Diana was no exception. I did say to everyone on arriving at the Abbey to take special care of themselves, as this location is not your average place. It is full of surprises, and those of mediumistic ability need to be even more careful as the spirits there have a tendency to have their way with you, whether you like it or not (as Diana found out!) I love Netley Abbey, even though it can scare the pants off me at times!'

Norie Miles, ghost investigator, *Out There Media*

The Ghosts of Netley

'By far the best proof is experience.'
Sir Francis Bacon – author, courtier and philosopher, 1561–1626

It was only after the event, much after, that I found out a little about what I may have experienced. It seems that there are a couple of ghosts that are said to wander the Abbey, and it seems like we had encountered both of them in the same night.

I'm sure you'll not be surprised to find out that one of the ghosts that is said to stalk the cloisters and corridors, is that of a monk: the Abbot, in fact. The Abbot is said to appear as a dark shadow, and is a strong and foreboding presence. It is said that this man committed many atrocities in his lifetime. I am told that some of these may have been connected to a woman who was some kind of servant in the building.

That leads nicely to our other spirit: the hag. There is no clear evidence of why a woman would be in the Abbey, but there she is. She is said to float between the rooms, and can often be felt.

I firmly believe that we encountered both of the known ghosts of Netley Abbey that night. Certainly, I am convinced that one of the voices on our digital recording was that of the unpleasant Abbot, and I am absolutely sure that the woman whose spirit tried to hijack mine was the female ghost that is often seen. There are (unsubstantiated) stories that the Abbot kept her as a virtual prisoner and tortured and abused her in every conceivable way. This would certainly explain her insanity, but there is no proof of this. In fact, there is no proof of the Hag of Netley Abbey at all. Whether she was a figment of my imagination or not; I can never be sure. I know the experience left me very shaken, and I have never forgotten it.

Face of the Keep

'Look in the face of the person to whom you are speaking, if you wish to know his real sentiments; for he can command his words more easily than his countenance.'
4th Earl of Chesterfield, Philip Dormer Stanhope

During my time as a ghost hunter I have been given the benefit of many people's opinions on what I do and what I *must* be like as a person. I have found that I am usually put into one of three categories:

- I'm a complete and total lunatic with no handle on reality;

- I'm a geek that likes fiddling with electronic equipment in my spare time;

- I'm a mercenary business woman that wants to put on a half-hearted show in order to make a hell of a lot of money ripping people off.

It is a shame that those who pass judgment on ghost hunters do not look a little further into what they do. For starters, many of the ghost hunts I have taken part in have not involved the general public, and most have been conducted for the interest of those present only: not for money.

Secondly, there are many charities that will vouch for the fact that ghost hunters contribute to their coffers on a regular basis.

One such charity is the *Freeman Hospital Children's Heart Unit Fund*, which is based in Newcastle. They were the recipients of a check for just under £1,500 from a charity ghost investigation at The Castle Keep, Newcastle-upon-Tyne, where I was one of the 'celebrities' that had been invited to take part.

Keep-ing the Faith

I had never been to the Keep before. Knowing little or nothing about the venue you are investigating is a distinct advantage for a medium. Contrary to popular belief, it does not help a psychic or medium to have prior information when giving any kind of reading or attempting to make contact with those who have passed on. Yes, it might be immensely helpful if you want to appear to be totally accurate; but in practice you may even fail to do that! What has been written on the internet or in books is not always fact. Many people forget this and those who are keen to impress – but short of moral fiber – often resort to a little advance research on the quiet. This is very short-sighted because if you read from the wrong site or book, you're in lumber before you start; let alone the moral implications of cheating in such a manner!

I had no desire to do any prior research. I believe that the only person you cheat is yourself. I was not even aware of the truly spectacular nature of the Keep until I got there.

Along with some of my colleagues for the night, we arrived at the Keep around 9pm. The Keep is stunning. From the very first look at it, staring up a flight of stone stairs to the enormous and imposing wooden door, I was entranced. I have been to many ancient buildings in my quest to search out spirits, but I was taken aback by the size and location of this impressive castle. I had been to Newcastle a few times before and was genuinely shocked I had never noticed such an incredible building. The stones oozed history and that history was spread over a varied site with arches, gateways and towers that were just crying out to be explored. I was eager to do that exploring and felt privileged to be there. It is easy enough to wander around ancient sites with a guide and fellow tourists during the day, but there is something magical about being able to do so overnight. History comes alive – and for me that is often a literal statement!

Castle Keep History

Although I was not privy to any history of the castle at the time, there is no reason to deprive you of it and it might help to give you some idea of the grandeur of the building and its incredible importance to the city of Newcastle.

The castle began its life in the second century as a Roman fort. It was built to protect the first bridge to cross the River Tyne: the *Pons Aelius*. First established as a castle in 1080, it was founded by the eldest son of William the Conqueror, Robert Curthose. In 1095 it passed over to the crown.

During the English Civil War, the Keep was repaired and fortified by the Royalist Mayor of Newcastle, Sir John Marley. Despite the fortifications, when the Scottish army crossed the border to support the Parliamentarians, the 1,500 strong garrison in the castle surrendered after a three month siege. This is possibly due to the fact that there were around 40,000 Scottish soldiers waiting outside for the garrison, and nothing to do with how secure the soldiers felt inside the castle's walls.

Between the 16th and 18th Century the Keep was used as a prison. During the 19th Century, rail travel came to Newcastle and a viaduct was constructed to the North of the Keep, crossing the site of the castle. Today, the East Coast Main Line railway runs through the grounds.

Settling In

Shortly after our arrival, we had the advantage of a brief tour with the castle custodian, Paul McDonald. I found out afterwards that Paul had been given strict instructions to only give information that was strictly necessary (such as which door leads where) to make sure that all the mediums present were not fed anything about the history of the Keep. After the tour, we met up with all the other attendees for the evening. As there were so many of us there, we were split into groups. This gave each group the ability to access all areas at least once, so that the whole of the building was covered.

At this point I should mention that although this investigation was used as a vehicle for raising money for charity, it was also conducted in a professional and serious manner. Regardless of the reason for the investigation, the organizers took the whole thing extremely seriously and were quite scrupulous in the way they dealt with both the mediums and the data they received via their numerous pieces of equipment.

I was put in a team with some key members of the *North East Ghost In-Specters* (now called the *North East Ghost Research Team)* as well as organizers, authors and paranormal investigators Darren W. Ritson and Mike Hallowell. As is the 'norm' for large investigations, we took one room and spent an allocated amount of time in it and then moved on to another room. I could probably write a small pamphlet on what happened at this one investigation. Suffice it to say that by the time we reached the Great Hall and the King's Chamber, we had already experienced some unusual phenomena, including inexplicable sounds on EVP recordings and odd temperature drops that seemed to manifest and disappear almost instantaneously.

As the night went on and we moved from one room to another, I had developed a real affection for my team. All of them seemed so professional and, even better, dependable. I have already attempted to get across the fact that I suffer from cowardice and that cold, spooky buildings do not help me with my affliction. You can imagine my relief that I was surrounded by people I felt would talk me out of my fear and keep me on track with what I was there to do – connect with the other side.

The King's Chamber

'The only thing I can't stand is discomfort.'
Gloria Steinem – American journalist, feminist and political
activist

I went into the King's Chamber accompanied by Darren, while
the others stayed outside in the Great Hall to take some
temperature and EMF readings. From the minute we set foot in
the chamber I felt uncomfortable. Although the room seemed
slightly brighter than the others and was certainly cozier and less
ruinous than most, I didn't like it at all. I can't tell you exactly
what I mean by that, because I was not sure at the time. It was like
a gnawing inside that tells you something is wrong and that
perhaps you should be somewhere else. Somewhere else that is a
very long way away from where you are right now. The stone
walls seemed to be moving in towards me although I knew that
they weren't. The empty space around seemed to be filled with
malice.

I simply couldn't shake the feeling. Everything around me
appeared to go out of focus for a moment and I wasn't quite sure
whether my eyes were playing tricks; whether I was feeling faint
and was a bit overtired, or whether the egg sandwich I'd had
earlier was about to vacate my stomach in the most colorful of
ways. The outer room seemed quiet, apart from the odd flash of
a digital camera or a mumble from some of the investigators in
there. No-one seemed at all perturbed. I did wonder if I was just
a bit rattled by the age, the cold and the creepiness of the rooms
we were in; but I'd been in so many similar places and hadn't
been affected by my surroundings very much before.

I have always been very aware of the importance of
communication with others around when things seem to be
going awry. I made a point of updating Darren on how I was
feeling, so that he could make a mental note and, quite possibly,

a written one. Darren was staring at me very intently as I spoke and his face ran the whole gamut of emotions from A to Z. It ended up fixed in a grimace.

As I finished my sentence, Darren started to spout a string of expletives. Up to this point I had had only a few conversations with Darren, but I had found him to be a passionate and professional paranormal investigator. I had also decided from observing him that if he met a 'man that you would not want to meet' in a dark alley, it would be that man that ran, not Darren.

Having come to this conclusion, I was amazed to hear him talk to me in an aggressive manner, fear showing in every feature on his face. He was shouting at me to get away from him (preferably in small, jerky movements, and preferably right now) and he was shaking with both anger and distress. I was honestly concerned that I had upset my host by admitting to being uncomfortable and this thought only added to my general unease. Darren seemed on a mission to cover as many four-letter words as possible and as loudly as possible and he was directing them all at me. I had to stare to be sure that these words were coming out of the mouth of a man who had earlier been so professional, courteous and supportive.

At this point Mike came into the chamber, startled by Darren's outburst and obviously concerned at what was, without a doubt, aberrant behavior. It was then that Darren decided to leave the room, hurriedly. Mike and I watched him disappearing, followed by his continuing string of expletives. He almost hit his head in his desperation to get away.

I was still feeling very odd within myself. I was upset by Darren's aggression but I also felt very dislocated and I looked at Mike for support. Mike stared at me intently for what seemed like hours (but was probably less than a minute) and then clarified the situation. Apparently, I had transfigured. I have mentioned in an earlier chapter that this means that the face of a spirit covers mine so that you can see the spirit clearly. Needless to say, many think transfiguration is a trick of the eyes; or some kind of auto-suggested hallucination caused by a 'spooky' environment. Those who've seen transfiguration for themselves tend to disagree with these opinions.

When Mike explained that I'd transfigured, I was surprised and concerned. I've experienced transfiguration a few times, but I've always felt 'something' before it happened; something more than a queasy stomach. In this case I had had no such warning and was not aware of any change, apart from the room looking odd for a moment. Let's face it – if you have the face of a spirit covering your own, you're not exactly going to see it for yourself, are you?

At this point, to his credit, Darren rejoined us in the King's Chamber. He had calmed down and was paying attention to what was happening. His string of expletives was no more, and the only thing that gave away his continuing discomfort was his pallor. This, to my mind, is the sign of a true professional in the field – someone who will run *at* what scares them – even if that means they are scared out of their wits when they do it.

By now, my nausea had increased and I was feeling frightened. I actually thought I might vomit at one point. I personally believe that the energies in the chamber had become so strong that it would have been possible for *anybody* to feel them. The most die-hard skeptic would have been sick to the stomach in the room, I'm sure. I knew there was something in there with us and I knew it was not nice. My senses told me it was a man: and he was certainly not a welcoming sort.

We all left the room then. The sick feeling had spread to Mike and Darren and had become debilitating for all of us. We stood just outside the room and attempted to pull ourselves together before we made another attempt at finding out what had just happened. We also wanted to determine if there *was* anything in the room other than a very unpleasant atmosphere. Although Mike and Darren both confirmed they had seen a spirit face over mine, they did not comment on what it had been. I told them that I had felt the spirit of a man around me – and they both nodded that it had been a man they had seen.

We braced ourselves and ventured back into the chamber, after updating the guys who were still studiously taking readings in the Great Hall. Mike got in first and I followed, with Darren behind me. Mike was only in the chamber a few minutes before he started to shake: he appeared to be having some kind of fit and both Darren and I were very concerned. However, Mike assured us that his reaction was to the spirit in the room rather than illness, and that he was being confronted by that spirit.

There seemed to be a battle of wills taking place and the outward signs of it were very hard to register logically. Mike seemed to be pushing against some invisible, immovable object and was staring intently at a spot in front of him. While this was happening I felt ill again, but I also felt very determined to be some kind of psychic (if not moral) support and stood my ground. I said to Mike that I could feel the spirit was trying to hit him or stab him in the stomach; but Mike finished the sentence with me as we both picked up the same thing. Mike finally stopped struggling with the empty air and regained his composure. He assured us that the spirit had left for a while. None of us really wanted to be there when he came back.

Witness Statement
'In early April 2006 I ran what was probably the biggest charity and celebrity paranormal investigation the North East of England has ever seen, at Newcastle Keep, for the Children's Heart Unit Fund. *Celebrities from the ghost hunting world, along with two other North East - based research teams, came together with* The North East Ghost In-Specters *(now called* The North East Ghost Research Team) *to investigate the ghostly goings on within these ancient castle walls.*

'Many well known faces in the paranormal world came and showed their support, including ITV2's Haunted Homes paranormal investigator Mark Webb, York's 'Ghost-Finder General' and historian, Rachel Lacy, and editor and writer for the spiritual and paranormal monthly publication Vision magazine, Diana Jarvis. Some of the top North East based writers and well-known ghost hunters were in also attendance too. Mike Hallowell, a freelance broadcaster and writer for Vision magazine attended. Mike has his own WraithScape column in the Shields Gazette, and has penned many books on the paranormal. He went on to investigate and co-write a book with me about one of the most well attested and most intense cases of poltergeist activity this country has ever seen; the South Shields Poltergeist.

'During the course of the charity investigation, many odd incidences occurred which were worthy of note. A number of strange EVPs were recorded, cameras refused to function in certain areas, and a very strange photograph was taken – which has caused some considerable debate – in the galleries area of the castle. There was, however, one incident that I was witness to that really made me think twice about psychic abilities, and how some spirits choose to communicate with the living. A short statement outlined below reiterates – in my words – what occurred to Diana on the night back in early April 2006.

'At 02.20am we entered the Kings Chamber. Diana stated more or less immediately that she was feeling very uncomfortable indeed; she did not like what she was feeling. At this point in the proceedings when I was talking to Diana, I noticed her face beginning to take on the form of what I presumed may have been an older spirit man. This episode lasted for about twenty or thirty seconds, and every time I looked back at her, the face was still the same. By' the face', I meant his.

'This scared me somewhat and I nearly ran into the door attempting to get away from it. What puzzled – and worried Diana – as she told me, 'is that when a spirit is close or when transfiguration is about to *occur, I am usually fully aware of it'. This time, however, she did not see or feel it coming and this concerned her. Mike Hallowell also caught the end of the transfiguration and he too agreed that her face was 'not hers'. It must be stressed that I personally did not believe in the idea of a spirit form showing itself through somebody's facial features, but after completing as many investigations as I have now, in many years of investigating, I have learned that anything can be possible.'*

Darren W. Ritson – author of *Ghost Hunter: True-Life Encounters from the North East*, and paranormal investigator

Of course, all of this must be so hard to believe. If you were not there with us to witness the alleged spirit face or feel the unpleasant energies in the room, why would you believe us? I, even now, find it difficult to accurately express how terrifying the whole event was and I find it even harder to rationalize. It is not a nice feeling to be told that your face has been borrowed and an even more unpleasant one to know that there is truth in the statement. I saw the look on Darren's face: Darren the immoveable, the unshakeable, the professional. I saw the battle that Mike had with thin air. If you had to choose someone to call a drama queen, Mike would be the last person on your list. If you met Mike in a bar and had a chat with him you would find him the most genial, knowledgeable and rational person – of that I have no doubt.

You must wonder what would possess intelligent, rational and realistic people to claim to have experienced such unbelievable things. I like to think that all three of us that were in the King's Chamber that night are intelligent, rational and realistic and that all three of us realize how totally fantastical our experience must be to someone who was not there. So why would we hold ourselves up for ridicule and regale you with our anecdotes of ghosts?

Many people *think* that a ghost hunter tells you of their experiences because they want you to buy into their belief structure. As mine changes on a regular basis, that would be hard anyway. Others think we are simply seeking attention. Neither assumption is true. We make our statements to obtain some degree of closure on them and also to allow others to make up their own minds about the possibilities of the paranormal. This book's aim is to do both.

'But in this world nothing is certain but death and taxes.'
Benjamin Franklin, American statesman, writer and inventor, 1706–1790

The Final Word

'Integrity is telling myself the truth. And honesty is telling the truth to other people.'
Spencer Johnson, author

Out of all the strange experiences I have had in my career as a ghost hunter, one of the most satisfying occurred at my own home, at one of the lowest points in my life. There were only two people present at the time this spirit visitation occurred: and that includes me. I think it's a fair bet that there would be no point attempting to track down the other witness to the event. He was scared (and probably humiliated) beyond belief and unlikely to be keen to relive it – or admit to it. I don't have any desire to speak to him, either. Read on and you'll see why.

Spirit Guides
There is a strong belief amongst those who work in psychic fields that everyone has a guide in spirit who helps us along life's path. They act almost as some kind of conscience – attempting to steer us away from the minefields we invariably walk into. Some believe we have several guides who help us with different areas of our life and I am certainly of the opinion that we have a few. If I look back over situations I have managed to extricate myself from, I must assume that I have had a small army of guides watching my back! Sometimes, despite the best efforts of our guides, we're just too stubborn or blinkered to see the mess we are getting ourselves into – and we push on regardless. In these

cases all our spirit guides can do is be there for us.

It took me many years to find out the identity of my 'main' spirit guide and many more to get used to her. Annaliese, a huge Danish woman from around the 10th Century, was so unlike me in personality it would take a positive effort to find two such dissimilar people. The only things we both shared were a sense of humor and a dislike of anything that could possibly record our body mass. She would appear in my mind's eye as an archetypal female Viking warrior, complete with horned helmet and blonde braids. I am convinced she did this only to tease me, as I have found no evidence that Viking women would really kit up like this. I don't tend to buy into Hollywood images.

Annaliese was clearly around primarily to help me with my psychic development, because she only turned up when I was working. I was not aware of her in my day-to-day life at all. As soon as I got some cards out, or started a ghost investigation, I could feel her presence behind me and to my left. There is only one occasion where she intervened in my daily life and this section is about that occasion. I will state for the record that I had never associated the word 'subtle' with Annaliese in any way; and I have her to thank for the huge collection of expletives that are now present in my vocabulary. I aim to avoid using them as much as possible, usually unsuccessfully.

As I write, I have the support of my new guide, Mackay; a drunken Scot that sits near the drinks cupboard in our kitchen, nursing a tumbler of single malt whiskey. Like Annaliese, he has a great sense of humor and he too uses the most colorful language. He also has the ability to pass on a message that means two things at once: and both interpretations are true. He took over where Annaliese left off. One day she just wasn't there anymore. Apparently, changes of guide are not uncommon, but that doesn't stop me missing my friend and support – the big Danish woman with the even bigger personality. Thanks to her I've learnt that sometimes, you really *do* have to say it like it is and euphemisms won't do.

Learning the Hard Way

'*It is better to suffer wrong than to do it, and happier to be sometimes cheated than not to trust*'
Samuel Johnson – writer, 1709–1784

Everyone will reach a time in their life when they realize – the painful truth slowly dawning – that they have made the most colossal error. It is at this point where my story starts. I had spent several years in a relationship, and that relationship had just reached its end. I am sure that my personal life is of interest only to myself and anyone who may have been involved in it, so I shall keep the description of my circumstances brief. Suffice it to say that the man in question had admitted to cheating on me (finally) and was in the process of setting up home with his new woman, who was carrying his baby. There was no question of reconciliation and frankly no point in it.

I have strange ways of dealing with pain. I rarely confront the person who's dealt it; as I see that as a waste of breath on someone who isn't worth it. I believe firmly that the best revenge is to live well. Not everyone shares my opinions – and I was about to find this out in the most dramatic way.

Because I don't do confrontation, I had just accepted my relationship was over and was busy trying to move on. However, I had not really grieved for the loss, or the pain, of finding out how I'd been used. My logical side concluded that it would be good for me to get some of the emotions out of my system that I had so carefully filed away and ignored. So one day, I contacted the man in question and told him that I desperately needed to talk to him one more time: but not with any idea of reconciliation, simply as a means of moving on and clearing the air. He knew me well enough to realize that I meant what I said, so he agreed to come over and see me.

I didn't really want to see him, though. I knew that for my health and sanity I should give him a piece of my mind; but I am not good at that. So, I befriended a bottle of wine who agreed to help me with the forthcoming confrontation. The wine and I became very good friends, and I had finished the bottle by the time my ex arrived.

It is never a good idea to drink too much and it certainly is not if you intend to conduct a ghost hunt; but that thought was so far away from my mind when I'd started nursing the bottle. For me, the evening was likely to be painful but healing – if it went to plan. Alcohol does not make a good supporting argument for a spirit encounter and I am quite happy if you want to file this particular event under 'she was drunk'. However, I can assure you it did happen and, as it offers such an insight into one of the more unusual ways spirit can help us here on the earth-plane, I'm going to include it. It's also very funny if you have had the misfortune of being wronged.

Now, back to our story, where I am reclined on a convenient sofa, after letting my ex into the house. He seemed as self-assured as usual and noticed that I'd had a drink or two, but didn't seem bothered. He stood opposite me as I tried to confront him about his behavior in an attempt at closure.

I have already mentioned that I am not good at confrontation. I should be clear and state that I am actually appalling at it. I hyper-ventilate if the situation becomes too bad and I perspire even before I've started (by now you will have noticed that I behave in a similar way in most difficult situations). Saying what I really, really think of someone does not come easily to me. I tend to use euphemisms to get across my point. I started to throw some euphemisms at my ex for starters and he listened, looking bored and distracted.

'You really shouldn't have done this, you know?' I offered. 'It was very unkind and it really hurt.'

'You ****,' said my inner self *'You didn't give a **** about me and*

I hope you drop dead.'

I heard the additional dialogue and studiously ignored it.

'When you behaved like this, it was very unfair,' I continued. 'Did you think about how it might make me feel?'

'You were a complete *******,' the internal dialogue continued *'and you didn't give a ****** **** about how I felt and I should have run you over at the first opportunity.'*

This internal and external series of statements went on for some time, with my ex occasionally attempting to justify himself as a reply. More often than not, though, I was making the statements to thin air while he ignored me. The more the very one-sided conversation went on, the more I realized that the additional comments had an accent: a very Teutonic accent. Through my foggy brain, I started to become aware of Annaliese standing behind me and realized that she was translating my rather wimpy accusations into versions that she seemed to think were more appropriate. The 'I' became 'you' and the sentences I heard became peppered with even more expletives.

My ex had, by now, become attentive. He looked at me strangely, but silently. Eventually, he asked me what was going on, as I seemed distracted. I told him that I had my spirit guide with me and he nodded. Spending seven years with me guarantees that you will take spirit guides and other miscellaneous psychic phenomena as a given.

I attempted to get back to leveling more wrongdoings at him. I had to keep stopping, though, to tell Annaliese to back off as I wanted to do this my way. She wasn't having any of it. Perhaps the drink contributed to my inability to push her away; or perhaps she was angry because I had been drinking, and was therefore more forceful. I was never much of a drinker and it is out of character for me to be under the influence.

Then the situation got out of control. I could feel her getting angrier and angrier and I couldn't even formulate a whole sentence without her adding her own narrative. I got cross and finally, I exploded. Not with my ex – the one person who deserved a bit of my righteous anger – no...I got cross with Annaliese.

'Back off!' I said. 'I'm going to do this my way and I'm not going to swear – I'm so much better than that.'

As I made this statement to both Annaliese and the room in general, I felt a change. The room shimmered, my ex's face seemed to drain of all color and I wobbled a bit. The next thing I knew I was sharing my space with another pair of eyes, another consciousness. Annaliese had become so frustrated by the situation she had pushed me aside (for the first and only time) and had taken me over. I had no fear of Annaliese and I simply felt a little dislocated, but I was still aware of everything that was going on. I was a bit miffed she'd just jumped in me like that, but I did find it hard to be cross with her as she had always been a loyal support to me.

What I was most aware of, though, was the look on my ex's face. He could see her. It was clear he was fully aware there were three people in the room. His mouth was open, his skin was pale and his eyes were wide. He looked like a rabbit caught in headlights.

I could feel Annaliese looking at him, through my eyes. To say that loathing accompanied her stare is an understatement. She despised him, of that I was in no doubt. I felt that she was looking at him in the same way a spider might contemplate a fly that had just stumbled, unwittingly, into her web.

I reiterated my previous statement to Annaliese - with some difficulty as I was no longer completely in control of all of my motor functions.

'I am not saying that to him, Annaliese. I am better than that.'

It seems that the repetition of my statement was the straw that broke the camel's back. I felt myself get up and draw myself to my full height. As I'm 5'2", that's not very impressive, but Annaliese was with me and I felt at least 6', both tall and wide. She stared at my ex some more, curling back her upper lip in disgust. He just looked at me / her...obviously terrified.

And then, without further ado, that wonderful woman said the one thing that needed to be said and the one thing that I had failed to realize until she said it. One sentence offered all the healing I'd ever need and gave me the closure that was so important.

I'm afraid I can't accurately describe in mere words how much venom was contained in what she said. I can tell you that she delivered her statement to him in a way that confirmed, without any room for doubt, that it was not me speaking. I can assure you that I was not the one that delivered the *coup de grâce* and you may, perhaps believe me. However, you will have to concede, if nothing else, that as a put-down it would be hard to find an equal.

'I am not saying that to him, Annaliese. I am better than that,' I whispered, repeating my previous statement.

Her eyes bored into him. She looked him up and down as if she was considering how something so revolting and insignificant had ended up before her. Then she delivered, full force and out loud, the words that embodied her passionate disgust of the man who had broken my heart and my life. She spat them at him so hard, and so pointedly, I wondered if he might fall back under their weight.

'Yes!' she said. 'You are *so* much better...than *that!*'

He ran. I had never seen him move so fast and I didn't realize he was capable of such speed. Before I knew it, the front door had closed and the house was empty of all but Annaliese and me. Although I couldn't see her face as he had done, I'm sure it had a satisfied grin on it. I felt her withdraw from me gently, almost apologetically, but I knew she felt triumphant.

I never saw *him* again. And, at last, I didn't care.

'Heav'n has no rage, like love to hatred turn'd,
Nor Hell a fury, like a woman scorn'd.'
William Congreve, English playwright and poet, 1670 – 1729

Taking Over

Possession is an emotive subject. When one thinks of possession, *The Exorcist* may spring to mind. This movie was allegedly based on a true story and shows the extreme measures taken by a group of Catholic priests to rid a young girl of a 'demon'. The girl exhibited the most unusual and disturbing phenomena, most of which could not possibly have happened under 'normal' circumstances.

However, possession is not necessarily as dramatic or upsetting as in the film. The events in this chapter bear no comparison to it; and in the case of Annaliese, the spirit concerned was being helpful. Not all possessions are demonic or harmful.

I would point out that I was never really in any danger during these experiences. Certainly, I was scared, but I came to no real physical harm and the spirits left me once they had made their presence felt. It seemed that the purpose of their visitations was simply to draw attention to their situation.

At Netley Abbey the woman had suffered immensely in her life. It is quite probable she wanted someone to know what had happened to her and that was why she used me as a vessel. It is also possible that she was so damaged mentally by her earthly life that she had not yet reached a stage where she was fully aware that her suffering was over and she could pass on.

At Newcastle Keep, the spirit concerned was unpleasant. He obviously did not want us there and the emotions that I felt when he 'possessed' me were of anger, but also of guilt. Was he hiding from the truth of what he'd done in his earthly life and just wanted to scare us away in case we found out?

Annaliese was simply cross and frustrated. She had tried to reason with me, but had failed to get the response she wanted. She was so concerned with my attitude (and aware that something needed to be done in order for me to heal) that she 'possessed' me in order to achieve a positive result for me.

Of course, these are just my thoughts and I *do* believe I was possessed, although not by any demon. I cannot offer *you* proof that a spirit invaded or shared my body and consciousness, but I can give you my thoughts on what happened. As ever, you will need to make up your own mind.

Chapter 8
Could You be a Ghost Hunter?

'And therefore as a stranger give it welcome.
There are more things in heaven and earth, Horatio,
Than are dreamt of in your philosophy.'
Hamlet Act 1, scene 5, 159–167

I said at the very beginning of this book that it is not my intention to convince you of the existence of ghosts. The experiences in this book are the most extreme I have had (and therefore, the most entertaining to read) and are, by their nature, hard to believe. If I was hoping that I might 'covert' some non-believers by offering my real-life experiences, I am intelligent enough to realize that these stories are unlikely to be the best choices I could make. My intention is not to convince you, though. It is to make you *think*.

When the question of belief (or not) of the afterlife arises, I have noticed that most people are very firmly in one camp or the other. However, objectiveness, or the pursuit of it, is essential in ghost hunting. If you are fascinated with ghosts and you want to delve further into the paranormal, you'll have to attempt to keep an open mind or you will be fooled by your experiences.

Even though I am a firm believer in alternative realities, I am not above being proven wrong about their existence. If you cannot see that another viewpoint to yours may be valid, your data will be biased, you will become entrenched in your beliefs, and you will be standing on the first step of the road that leads to evangelism. With every experience in this book, there is an alternative argument to the one that I have proffered. Perhaps:

- I was tired and hallucinated;

- I saw something odd and my mind added the rest, as it did not have any other solution to what was happening;

- My eyes, and my mind, were playing tricks with me.

It is essential that you are able to accept other possibilities because then you can explore more thoroughly what really did happen. The minute we state something as absolute fact; that 'fact' will be scrutinized. It is essential that you are fully prepared for someone to play Devil's Advocate and I would recommend you have someone in your ghost hunting team that can do so effectively.

Ghost hunting is an absorbing hobby, but it is not for everyone. If you are quick to assume that every noise out of place is a ghost – don't do it. If you think the whole notion of the human spirit existing after death is bunkum – you'll not get much satisfaction from a ghost hunt and you'll be seen as narrow-minded.

The main prerequisites for a ghost hunter are:

- The ability to laugh at yourself;

- A scientific approach;

- An open mind;

- Patience;

- Determination;

- Stamina;

- A fairly empty social calendar.

If you've got to this point in the book and I've failed to put you off the idea of ghost hunting, then I hope you will find what you are looking for. If you are looking for conclusive, scientific proof that ghosts exist, I suspect you are in the wrong field or have set your hopes a bit high. If you want to spend your time at ghost hunts, laughing at the 'poor fools' that believe in spirits...you need to get out more.

However, if you are hoping that you may learn more about life (and death) and have some fun on the way, you would be hard pushed to find a more rewarding hobby.

> *'Anyone who takes himself too seriously always runs the risk of looking ridiculous; anyone who can consistently laugh at himself does not.'*
> Vaclav Havel, Czech Playwright and President of Czechoslovakia (1989 – 92)

About the Author

Diana Jarvis is a Capricorn, born on 10th January 1964. She lives with Gordon, her husband, as well as the spirits of an old lady and a tom cat – both of whom haunt the master bedroom in her house. The cat sprays periodically, just to make sure she knows it's 'his' room and, although his habit is smelly, it doesn't last long and spirit stains require little in the way of cleaning.

She has a step-son called Jonathan, a step-daughter called Fai and two sons of her own: Robert and David. All of her children think she's mad and all of her children are almost certainly right. She spends her spare time giving psychic readings; cooking; cross-stitching and reading. She also dresses up in 17th Century clothing and re-enacts battles from the English Civil War by firing large, operational cannons at 'Parliamentarian' soldiers.

She has taught Tarot, Runes, Wicca, Mediumship, Paranormal Investigation Techniques and Spiritual Development; appeared on a plethora of TV channels, radio stations and in magazines; lectured on a variety of subjects from ghost hunting to candle magick and has appeared on a breakfast television program as a Klingon in order to teach singer Robbie Williams the niceties of the language. Her success in the last of these endeavors is questionable and its connection with the subject matter of this book is non-existent.

Her main ambition is to raise enough money to move to an old farmhouse in the Limousin, France…and to keep chickens.

'If my doctor told me I had only six minutes to live, I wouldn't brood. I'd type a little faster'.
Isaac Asimov, science fiction author, 1920–1992

B O O K S

O is a symbol of the world, of oneness and unity. In different cultures it also means the "eye," symbolizing knowledge and insight. We aim to publish books that are accessible, constructive and that challenge accepted opinion, both that of academia and the "moral majority."

Our books are available in all good English language bookstores worldwide. If you don't see the book on the shelves ask the bookstore to order it for you, quoting the ISBN number and title. Alternatively you can order online (all major online retail sites carry our titles) or contact the distributor in the relevant country, listed on the copyright page.

See our website www.o-books.net for a full list of over 500 titles, growing by 100 a year.

And tune in to myspiritradio.com for our book review radio show, hosted by June-Elleni Laine, where you can listen to the authors discussing their books.

MySpiritRadio